PUPPALICIOUS AND BEYOND

LIFE OUTSIDE THE CENTER OF THE UNIVERSE

PF HUTCHINS

SKIPJACK PUBLISHING.COM

FREE EBOOKS

Before you begin reading, you can snag a free Pamela Fagan Hutchins ebook starter library by joining her mailing list at.https://pamelafaganhutchins.com/sign-up-for-pamela-fagan-hutchins-author-newsletter/.

I AM NOT A WHACKJOB.

{Before you start, you can snag an exclusive, free Pamela Fagan Hutchins' *What Doesn't Kill You* mystery novella by joining her mailing list at http://eepurl.com/lq-bP, if you wanna.}

I am not some whacko who writes about her labradoodle Schnookums. Let's just get that straight right off the bat. Hell, I'm practically anti-animal, and I don't believe in the Loch Ness Monster, either. Dogs? They shed. Poop. Pee. Barf. Drool. Chew. Bark. Cats? Ditto, except make that yowl instead of bark, plus I'm deathly allergic. That's why currently we have only three dogs and one cat. Oh, and five fish. And I hardly even like them, except for maybe a little. We've cut back, too. It wasn't so long ago the dog count was six, the cat count three, and the fish count innumerable, along with guinea pigs, birds, ducks, rabbits, and a pig. As in swine.

My most vivid memories of growing up in Wyoming and Texas are of animals. We had the normal sorts of pets, plus the absolute luxury of living in the country. I raised sheep for 4-H and rode my horse to sleepovers. We had visitors furry, feathered, and scaly, of both the hooved and clawed varieties. My husband grew up on St. Croix where the animals were different, but his wild upbringing, close to nature, matched mine. His mother tells stories of her sons bringing geckos on the plane from the island to the mainland, and finding their little skeletons outside the family's summer home in Maine months later. Eric's favorite photograph from his youth shows him standing on the beach holding the booby he rescued while surfing, then nursed back to health and released.

As a child, I devoured books about animals, like *Black Beauty* and *Where the Red Fern Grows.* I idolized James Herriot and Jacques Cousteau. I could never quite decide whether to be a veterinarian or a marine biologist or Shamu's trainer. Somehow I sold out early on and became a lawyer, but that didn't stop the animal love. There, I've admitted it: animal love. I ♥ animals, with a big red heart and sparkly glitter. All of them, nearly, except for maybe insects and reptiles. Also I am not a big fan of rats. But other than that, I love every one. Eric and I spend all the time we can outdoors looking for critters, whether we do it from bicycles or cars, or in the water or on our own four feet. We watch *All Creatures Great and Small* on Netflix. Our offspring naturally love God's creatures, too, at least as much as they love their smartphones, and a whole lot more than they love us.

In the Virgin Islands of Eric's youth, Christianity made plenty of room for the ghosts, spirits, and jumbies of obeah, a folk-magic religion with elements of sorcery and voodoo. The locals couldn't comprehend why continentals like me scoffed at what was so plainly true to them, but scoff I did. Ghosts? Jumbies? As in Casper the friendly? It was hard for me to follow—until I met Eric. He and the islands opened my eyes to a world that existed just beyond the visible. Sometimes these non-humans scared me, and sometimes they comforted me. I liked my pets and the animals of the wild better, but I was captivated by the jumbies. Especially the one guarding Annaly, the house we bought in the rainforest.

When my lawyer career morphed into human resources and then I finally started writing, non-humans started spilling out of every story. Sometimes they are the stars, and sometimes they are the supporting actors. No matter their role, they always manage to steal the show from the unsuspecting humans who believe they are the center of the universe.

PART ONE: CREATURES CARIBE

FROGGY WENT A'COURTIN'

All the signs were there. We even talked about them, way back when. "The owners must love frogs," Eric said as we toured the back yard of the house in Houston that would become our home when we left the islands. He nudged a knee-high pottery frog planter with his foot.

"Umm hmmm," I said. I couldn't have cared less. I was calculating our offer.

"That one is odd," he said. He pointed at a large concrete frog Buddha, almost hidden by giant elephant ears and bougainvillea beside the waterfall that poured from the top pond into the middle one. You could see the ponds all the way from the front door, through the seamless full-length back windows. It reminded us of home, of St. Croix in the U.S. Virgin Islands, of our beloved rainforest home Estate Annaly. How could we not buy this house? Eric continued, "It's like a frog shrine."

I remember saying something noncommittal, like, "Whoa, that *is* odd," as I walked back into the house with the real estate agent. In retrospect, she seemed . . . in a hurry.

We moved in on the ninth of March, springtime in Houston. Beautiful springtime. For roughly six weeks, the temperatures are in the seventies and there's a soft breeze. Flowers bloom but mosquitoes don't yet. Sunlight dapples the ground through the vibrant foliage of the trees. Birds don't chirp, they sing. The fragrance is clean, more than sweet. It's heaven. We moved in, and our new house was like heaven.

Until everything arrived from the islands in another month, we had exactly one piece of furniture: a standard double mattress on the master bedroom floor. The kids slept in sleeping bags. It was spare. We ate our meals on paper plates sitting cross-legged on the floor. When we called to each other, our voices bounced from wall to wall in our 4,000-square-foot echo chamber. Still, it was like heaven.

But around midnight during our fateful third week in Houston, the first frog croaked. His piercing rasp drew our attention, but not our consternation. What was one frog to us, here in heaven?

Oh, had it only been one frog. Or one hundred frogs. Or even one thousand. By three a.m., Eric was standing pondside in his skivvies with three hundred pounds of canine looky-loos beside him in the forms of Cowboy the giant yellow Lab, Layla the Gollum-like boxer, and Karma the emotionally fragile German shepherd. I stood in the doorway.

"F*&^ing frogs," Eric said, no trace of love in his voice.

Well, yes. Yes, they were. Frogs were, ahem, *fornicating* everywhere. It was overwhelming, really. I swear, if you'd Googled "swingers' resort for frogs," you'd get our address. The amorous amphibians held their tongues as soon as Eric switched on the backyard light. Muttering more curses, he snatched them up in stubbornly conjoined pairs and flung them over the fence. I did not dare ask his plan and after ten minutes, I sneaked off to bed.

Night after sleepless spring night, Eric battled the frogs with a homicidal drive. Day after spring day, he shirked his work as a chemical engineer and looked online for ways to off them. This campaign was beginning to drive me insane, too. Their sounds had long since become white noise, or at worst, bedtime music to me. Eric's tossing, turning, cursing, and trips in- and outside, on the other hand, kept me wide awake. He would report the body count when he returned to bed.

"If I could just think of a way to poison them, I could sleep," he said.

"If you poison them, you'll poison the dogs, maybe even birds," I said into my pillow.

"Acceptable collateral damage," he replied.

In response to my urgings for him to quell his frog-blood lust, Eric tried to repatriate his little nemeses. He loaded them into industrial-sized black garbage bags and headed for the bayou. Unfortunately, the good citizens of Houston were on alert for a serial murderer that spring, and a man seen dumping lumpy garbage bags into the waterway attracted attention. Eric had only just barely returned home before the cops came to check him out. Reluctantly, I vouched for him.

The kids got into the spirit. Instead of just one underwear-clad man in the back yard, we now had him (thank the Lord, he'd started taking the time to don a pair of camo shorts—although I had the feeling he'd spring for camo face and body paint, too given the chance) plus the nine-, eleven-, and thirteen-year-old kids. Like me, the dogs were sleeping through most of it now, except when one of the kids would make a particularly good snatch and yell in triumph. At least it was taking care of any lingering need for sex education.

When the children created an offering of dead froggies to the Buddha, I feared the repercussions. And maybe it was my imagination, but I could swear their numbers doubled that night. It was bad. It was very, very bad.

It pains me to admit that I conspired by my silence in the deaths of hundreds of croakers that spring. They died in an endless variety of ways, but mostly Eric heaved them—THUMP, or occasionally SPLAT—against the house. Sometimes he aimed high, and more than once we found dead frogs clear on the other side of the house the next morning, or their desiccated bodies on the roof weeks later.

"Maybe I should have let the cops take you after all," I groused one night as he stomped off. The man seemed by God determined to ensure that I shared his insomnia.

"What?" he said.

"Maybe I should come out and help you after all," I said, and got out of bed. Ugh.

The calendar pages flipped slowly forward. May passed. It wasn't seventy degrees anymore. The flowers wilted and the mosquitoes hatched. A faint smell of decay—mold?—permeated the house, but it smelled no better outside. The sun burned everything in its searing gaze, yet still the frogs croaked out their horny croaks and gamboled nightly in sexual abandon.

"They'll be gone by summer," I said, certain that they would not. That they would never leave. That my husband would be scribbling *REDRUM* across our bathroom mirror by August while the frogs croaked on. Because "frogicide" written backward doesn't spell anything.

And then one day, they stopped. Silence. Sleep. Happiness. Months went by, blissful days leading inevitably toward April. *Make the clock move slower*, I prayed to God.

January. February. March. We hadn't heard them yet, but the little fockers would be here soon. Apri-ri-ri-RIBBITTTTTTT. Eric leaped up in bed as if the frogs were in there with him.

"Honey, stop," I said.

He glared at me. All my man could see was frogs.

I handed him a pair of earplugs that I'd scavenged a few weeks before from his bag of work safety wear. "It's evolutionary, honey, Darwinian. If our species is to survive, we must adapt."

He stared at them, foamy yellow plugs on either end of a neon-orange string. I took his hand, placed them in his palm, and gently closed his fingers around them. I tugged him out of bed and led him out into our humid back yard, picking up a candle and matches on the way. I left the outside lights off and the male frogs sang out in carnal frenzy. I felt primal, like I was entering a hedonist temple.

Before the frog Buddha, I knelt with my husband. I handed him the candle and matches, then nudged him when he didn't respond. "Light it, my love." He did, a penitent virgin on the altar. He lit the candle. "Now, repeat after me," I said.

He mumbled assent and I began. "I, Eric, present myself before you, Buddha of the frogs."

The look he shot me said, "You're out of your flippin' gourd," but I didn't waver, and he repeated my words.

"I promise to do no harm to any of your frog brothers and sisters, henceforth and forevermore."

"I'm not saying that," he said.

"Humor me. We did it your way all last summer," I said. *And honey, I'm voting you off THAT island, I thought.*

He complied with the enthusiasm of Morticia Addams.

"As a token of my sincerity, I pledge to you to wear these earplugs, and to install a frog shrine in our bedroom immediately."

He repeated the oath, then we blew out the candle and tiptoed in perfect solemnity back into our room. There, I pulled two jolly stuffed frogs from a bag and propped them up on a pedestal table by the back window, between Eric and the live frogs.

"You actually went out and bought these in advance?" he asked.

"I knew I had to take matters into my own hands. I love you, and I want our marriage to withstand the test of frogs."

"It's that bad, huh?"

"Oh yeah, it's that bad."

Eric finally—FINALLY—smiled and swatted me on the behind. He put the earplugs in.

"Those are kind of sexy," I said.

"What?" he yelled.

Mission accomplished.

CREEPY CRAWLIES AND THINGS THAT GO BUMP IN THE NIGHT

I lived in the U.S. Virgin Islands for six years, and the critters of the Caribbean kinda creeped me out. I didn't go all nutso about it like Eric did with the frogs, but they left their mark on my psyche.

Most people envision tropical tranquility when I tell them I met and married my husband on St. Croix, but not everything in paradise is idyllic. Don't get me wrong: it's gorgeous, and we loved it. But some of God's little creations in the U.S.V.I. make you wonder if He is related to Tim Burton. And this coming from a woman who grew up with rattlesnakes, black widows, water moccasins, copperheads, and scorpions in Texas.

In the water, the animals of the V.I. are lovely. I adore the puffer fish. My eyes devour the vivid colors of the parrot fish. How much more beautiful can something get than the eagle ray? Sure, there are underwater beasts that sting like a jellyfish or bite like a barracuda, but not often. On land, though, on land, you get only the scrubs who can survive in desert-like island conditions. For instance, you have the gungalos.

Gungalos are large millipedes with glossy red or black exoskeletons that are filled with acid. That's right, acid. And they propagate like rabbits. Worse than rabbits. Worse than the *frogs.*During the nearly year-round gungalo season, people have to sweep up gungalos from their floors and patios multiple times a day. Did you catch that? I said floors, as in the floors in your house. Because in the V.I., most people live in open-air settings, meaning their doors and windows remain open more often than not. The gungalos—and other creepers—make themselves right at home. Thus, you won't just find them on your floor. You'll find them on your bed and in your shoes, too. If you step on a gungalo, you'll hear a nasty crunch and then see an ooze the color of the exoskeleton, which is either black or reddish. If you're barefoot, it stings. The ooze leaves a stain on your foot or the floor for as long as a month. Eric bought his first skateboard from the penny-per-gungalo his parents used to pay him to sweep, bag, and dispose of them.

Joining the ranks of the proud and the poisonous are the geckos. Geckos are heroes that eat the no-see-ums. No-see-ums are tiny gnats that get their name because, well, you can't see them. But you know they've been there because they leave their calling card: a stinging bite. I spent my first six months on-island in scabby welts from no-see-ums. They feasted on my tenderfoot skin. I still have a scar from a particularly nasty bite. After a while, I guess I developed immunity or a stench they didn't like, and they left me alone.

Back to the geckos. Geckos eat insects, but they can get into anything, anywhere. We would find their little lizard poos all over the place, and once during a dinner party we saw their skeletons under the glass top of our dining room table in a hidey-hole we had missed when cleaning. Not appetizing. Our cats loved the geckos. They loved to chase them, to torment them, and to eat them. However, geckos are mildly poisonous when consumed. Our cat Juliet knew this from firsthand experience. You could tell poor kitty had eaten too many geckos when she started to weave around and foam at the mouth. I've never known it to be fatal, but I've seen a lot of gecko-drunk felines.

Also poisonous? Centipedes. Evil, evil centipedes. Centipedes still haunt my dreams. In theory, I was familiar with centipedes from pre-island life. But it wasn't until I moved to St. Croix that I understood what horrible creatures they are. They *are*Satan in his living form. Don't believe me? Try waking up to a six-inch black and yellow monster in bed with you, latched on for a nice bite on your neck. Been there, done that. The bite alone is painful enough to get your attention, but it's what comes next that's truly demonic: swelling, stinging, nausea, numbness, fever and dizziness. It's dangerous to small children and people with allergies, who can go into anaphylactic shock. In six years in the islands, I was bitten three times. My husband, in his forty years there, was only bitten twice. Like all the other island pests, we could keep them at bay but not eliminate them completely, even with regular visits from Terminix. Once I was able to kill a large one without mauling its colorful body, so I left it on Eric's pillow as a surprise. After I peeled him off the ceiling, he said he liked it better when I surprised him with fishnet hose and a garter belt.

Leaving the poisonous and moving on to the obnoxious, the island toads send me into dry heaves, even actual heaves. My parents battled toads for several years in their house on St. Croix, which was named Whispering Palms {Prior to realizing they would become his in-laws, my husband dubbed their home Farting Bushes. Tsk, tsk, not nice.} for the coconut palms lining its ridge. At Whispering Palms, the rooms were connected by exterior covered breezeways that were lined on either side with planter beds. The toads would emerge from the soil at night and stand in stacks upon each other, five deep in some places. From what I could tell, they came out solely to piss my mother off by crapping all over the hallways, but possibly they also emerged to eat and engage in recreational sex. My mother is not a fan of casual sex or toads.

It gets worse. Tap water, in the islands, usually comes from below-house cisterns that are filled by roof catchments. You control your own water quality with additives and filters. Occasionally a homeowner might have a reason to get into the cistern. Eric and I had five separate cistern chambers below Annaly, and a few of them were only accessible by going down a ladder into one chamber and, depending on the water level, walking, swimming, or rafting into another. In the dark. But I digress. So, back to Whispering Palms. My father had to get into their cistern for one reason or another, which he had not done in quite some time. To his horror, he discovered hundreds—possibly thousands—of the breezeway toads, pooping, peeing, fornicating, and God knows what else in the depths below their house, into their bathing and drinking water.

Did you just throw up a little? That's okay. I did, too.

I like the tree frogs much better than the toads. The tree frogs are native to Puerto Rico and known as "coqui" (ko-kee), because that's the sound they make (all night long). They are darling little quarter-sized creatures. They are usually green, at least on St. Croix, but I've seen them in a range of colors that match their surroundings. They may be cute, but the coqui lullaby becomes water torture after four or five sleepless nights.

And then there are the island sparrows, AKA bats. Initially, they wigged me out. We had, no lie, hundreds living under the eaves at our rainforest house. They would slip out of their attic hideaway at dusk, two or three at a time, to hunt for bugs and to take sips of water out of our swimming pool. After a while, I came to appreciate them for their appetite for mosquitoes, and because it was perfectly lovely to sit on the patio in the evenings and watch them swoop and flutter. Banish your thoughts of bloodthirsty vampire bats—these flying mammals would almost fit in your palm. However, I admit I didn't like it when they got inside the house. Once there was a bat on the ceiling of our bedroom that I had to chase out with a tennis racket. When I couldn't get it all the way outside, I managed to trap it under a beach bucket and then gently walk the bucket to the porch, where I released it.

Above: Cutie-pies in the garage.

So, I didn't resort to bagging bats and dumping them on the beach like so many frogs into the bayou, but I do have recurring nightmares of a foot-long centipede stinging me into paralysis in my bed, where I lie immobile, tortured by the cry of the coqui and covered in gungalos and geckos, watching towers of toads poop on my clean floors.

Love 'em or hate 'em, the land critters of the Caribbean make an impression.

GUARD DOG IN TRAINING

When I first bought Annaly, we had to sic the contractors on it for about six months before it was habitable. That gave me time to prep the family—kids and pets alike—for the radical lifestyle change ahead of us. Cowboy, our yellow labrador, was only one year old. Young Cowboy needed to develop some skills before he could become the alpha guard dog. I had my doubts the big goofball was cut out for the job.

My brother Bruce visited us about halfway through the finish-out. After showing him our progress, the kids and I set out from Annaly toward my favorite place in whole world: the tidal pools. The hike to the tidal pools was rugged. The rainforest terrain of the island's north coast was steep, and the trail was thick with saw grass in some places. My kids were youngish, too; Susanne was nearly seven and Clark was nine at the time. Cowboy came with us, because he went everywhere Susanne went, except school, and he would have gone there, too, if we'd let him.

It took us an hour to reach the pools, where we picnicked before our swim. We all got a belly laugh out of watching Cowboy follow Susanne through the water at first. He was a powerful swimmer, as you would expect for a labrador. Oh, to have the slightly webbed toes and buoyancy of a lab. We realized, though, that he might drown her in his urgent need to be near her, so with our coaching she got behind Cowboy and held onto his collar. He dragged her around the pools as if she was weightless, and I swear he was smiling.

Then Clark and Susanne decided to jump into the water from the low rock cliffs around the pool. It was a great idea, in theory. First Clark climbed up and jumped. That went fine. Then it was Susanne's turn.

Susanne climbed the slippery, steep rocks. This didn't bother me until Cowboy, who weighed twice as much as Susanne, noticed where she'd gone. He dug his toenails into the rock and somehow hauled his one hundred and ten pounds out of the water by his front legs. He scrambled up the rocks like a drunken mountain goat. Susanne stood poised for her jump as he closed in on her fast.

"Jump, Susanne, jump NOW," I screamed. The collision between dog and small girl wasn't going to be pretty, and there was no way I could get to her in time.

She looked back at the barreling figure of Cowboy and for once in her young life didn't ask, "Why, Mommy?" She leaped into the water a few seconds before Cowboy reached the spot on which she had been standing. He whined, he moaned, he thrashed his head side to side. Susanne surfaced, laughing.

"Swim to me as fast as you can, honey, as fast as you can," I urged, trying not to panic. Now I was picturing his body, claws first, landing on her head.

Susanne had joined the swim team at the age of five, and she put all that training to good use at the right moment. She shot toward me as Cowboy swan-dived off the rock face. He landed with four legs splayed in a furry cannonball. His splash propelled Susanne the last few feet to me.

Not to be deterred from the object of his adoration, he swung his giant muzzle back and forth until he locked eyes on her. He engaged his powerful dog paddle.

"Now, darlin', you know what to do." And she did.

Susanne waited until Cowboy was three feet away, then she dove under water, coming up behind him. She grabbed his collar.

"Good boy," she yelled.

My pulse, which had triple-timed during the last forty-five seconds, slowed down as dog dragged daughter around the tide pool. Clark splashed in the shallows, oblivious to the drama. Bruce had appeared by my side without me noticing until now. We exchanged a long look.

"That dog is a little protective," he said.

"I knew he was crazy about her, but that was more than I expected," I said.

"Again!" Susanne yelled.

"No, ma'am!" I yelled back.

On the hike back out, Cowboy ratcheted up his attention to Susanne and kept station off her flank like a sheepdog. If one of us got between dog and girl, he simply shoved us back out of the way, no matter how steep or narrow the path. We passed some other hikers and he emitted a low rumble as they passed his girl. It was a long hike, and we were all pretty tired. Several times, Susanne stopped for an ugly mood swing, but Cowboy would herd her back into forward motion.

"Good boy," I said, and patted his head. He didn't take his golden eyes off Susanne to acknowledge my praise. It looked like the guard dog was almost ready for life in the rainforest.

GHOSTIES, GHOULIES, AND LONG-LEGGEDY BEASTIES

I may not believe in zombies, sparkly vampires, or Bigfoot, but I do believe in something. I know there's more out there than my eyes can see or my outer ear can hear. I feel it sometimes. I sense it. Do you? There's an energy around us, inhabiting an invisible dimension.

Some people never sense it. Others have what I think of as an extrareceptive ear, a greater capacity to relate to the energy around us, like the energies from living people, from animals, or even from formerly living people. From a million unseen, unheard sources, some that we can't name, but we know exist.

Culture plays a role. In some parts of the world, kids are raised to believe, and so they listen more openly. Eric grew up in the Caribbean, where jumbies—ghosts, spirits—were an accepted and expected part of life. Santería, voodoo, and other tropical-clime practices exist for a reason. People in the islands look for ways to communicate with and harness the power of spirits. Eric has this receptivity, this special ear, and he really freaked me out at first when he sensed the presence of something that wasn't actually living among us, like he did immediately at Annaly.

I've got some sort of this sensitivity. I could feel the jumbie at Annaly, too. But I'm a bit more of an empath. You know, like Deanna Troi in the purple jumpsuit on *Star Trek: Next Generation*. That kind of empath. Whether chemically or by my thoughts, when I'm with someone in person, I can get all the way through to them, and I receive much more in terms of energy and connection from them than most other people do.

Yeah, yeah, I know. You think this is crap. But it isn't. People understand and relate to me, latch onto me, grab hold of the energy I put toward them. It makes me a heck of an investigator, executive coach, and public speaker—things I do in my day job—but I don't always want to go there. It takes a lot out of me. And when I knowingly open my channel, people that are too needy can almost incapacitate me. I've learned to protect myself, protect my resources.

The closer I am emotionally to a person, the more powerful this force can be. I can connect from longer distances with those to whom I am closest. And of course, the more the other person is in touch with the unseen, the greater the energy we can pass between us. I think my husband's similarity to me in this regard was one of the things that drew us together originally, back when we were co-workers and there was no twinkle of forever in our eyes yet.

Eric was once in a horrific bike wreck while I was ten miles away, cooking dinner up at Annaly. Suddenly I was hit by a blunt force of traumatic energy that sent me down on my knees with my hand around my throat. I grabbed my car keys and mobile phone off the counter without so much as my purse or an idea of where I was heading. I drove at breakneck speed toward town. Fifteen minutes later, when I was out of the rainforest and back into cell reception, my phone rang. It was Eric. He had hit a car head-on and was refusing medical treatment. He had woken with no memory of who he was but kept saying he needed Pamela. And I had heard him.

If humans have this much energy to tap into the unseen with each other, doesn't it stand to reason that we can sense, feel, and hear the other unseen energies around us? I believe all of this energy is interconnected and constant, that some auras are just so powerful that through their force and circumstances, they can't easily be erased. It's not like I think there are bajillions of undead spirits clamoring for me to hear them, but I *know* some spirits outlast their physical bodies. They're out there. I know they are. Just because I can't see them to name them doesn't make their presence less tangible.

And how do you explain some people's greater intuition about things—spatial relations and connections to the energy emanating from objects? I am attuned, but my inner ear works best on living (and maybe formerly living) things. Eric is attuned, as is his son. My daughter Susanne is, too, but she has an inner ear that functions differently than mine. Suz has a tremendous relationship to animals and objects. She is a Dog Whisperer with the soul of a cat.

She has another skill that is stranger, though: Susanne knows where things are. The first few times she knew without looking where I had left, for instance, the camera ("In the upstairs closet on the top right shelf, Mom"—the *"duh"*was implied), I attributed it to nosiness. Surely she had just pawed through the closet and run across it? But we noticed she knew immediately where things were when we asked, and her only explanation for it was "I just know." She keeps a good visual inventory of her surroundings. For instance, she goes through my drawers almost daily and will announce at dinner, "So, you got new panties, I see," apropos of nothing. It transcends observation (and nosiness), though, into the realm of the relational energy stored in objects. If we lose something, we ask her. If it's findable, she knows where it is. If she says it's gone, she's right, and we give it up as truly lost.

Thus, with this belief in the unseen, I write. And they, whatever it is they are, make their way into my stories. My nonfiction is full of it. Okay, that came out wrong, but you get my point. My fiction is, too. Most of my fiction is grounded in memory, anyway. What is fiction, after all, but life reimagined? Life, only more interesting. Life, with the answer to "what if?" If you've read my nonfiction, you'll recognize my fictional characters like old friends you've never met, and I'm going to introduce you to them in this book.

So it's not just the animals that vie for center stage in the theater of my words. It's also the jumbies. And let's meet one now, in an adapted excerpt from my novel *Saving Grace.*

FINDING ANNALISE

Adapted excerpt from the novel *Saving Grace (Katie #1)*:

I guess you could say I chose to drown the sorrow of my unrequited love in a hundred and ten acres of bush and six thousand square feet of partly-finished house in a tropical island rainforest.

Her name was Annalise, or rather, Estate Annalise. A crook had begun to build her years before and abandoned her, half-complete, when the Feds invited him to spend time in one of their correctional institutions. Word has it that he told his friends he was going to visit his mother. The next thing you know, his picture was on the cover of the *San Juan Star*. "St. Marcos Man Convicted as Drug Kingpin," the headline blared. This explained his boat, plane, and houses on several islands; just another Caribbean success story, so to speak.

Annalise, the house he built and left, was a jumbie house. A jumbie, in West Indian folk magic like voodoo or Santeria, is a ghost or spirit.

Completely bonkers, right? Only it wasn't.

I discovered Annalise while I was on a trip to St. Marcos. My name is Katie Connell—a good Irish Catholic name for a Baptist girl from Texas—and I have the red hair, pale skin, volatile temper, and family history of alcoholism you'd expect. I ran to St. Marcos to spend two weeks at a spa there as a form of self-rehabilitation. AA may work for most people, but I don't do group activities very well. Besides, I'd merely been drinking too much for too long a time; I was not an alcoholic.

The only thing I wanted from St. Marcos was serenity, and to prove to my brother Collin that I could give up Bloody Marys for two whole weeks. Finding Annalise was an accident. Or maybe it was fate.

So, there I was on St. Marcos, at a resort that promised a wide variety of island adventures for the guests that weren't into the chichi spa services. Guests like me. I laced up my boots and set out for a guided hike in the rainforest led by Rashidi Johns. It sounded like the kind of "take me away from myself" adventure I needed.

Rashidi was a botanist by education, an entrepreneur by nature, and a Rastafarian by faith. His neatly-tied dreadlocks hung all the way to his waist. He was lean from his vegetarian life, but strong. The female hikers found him exotic and appreciated his dark physique. Due to his popularity, the group I joined for the morning hike was sizable.

Rashidi walked through the tittering throng, checking us for appropriate clothing, footwear, sunscreen, bug spray, hats, and hydration. He sent a few women back for supplies, and one or two he delicately queried about their constitutions and health.

"The rainforest on St. Marcos is one of the most beautiful places in the world, but it is rugged, ladies, and it be harsh." His calypso accent was thick, but understandable. "There may be some of you that would enjoy it more with a drivin' tour. These hills are steep. The sun is brutal. There are centipedes as long as me foot." Someone laughed. "I not jokin' you, ladies. You will see beautiful trees, blossoms and vines, but dey can reach out with their t'orns and stickers and tear your soft skin. They grow t'ick togedder, so at times I will be using this," he patted the machete strung across his hip, "to clear a path for us to get t'rough. You ain't going to make me sad if you decide this hike is not for you. I can only carry one of you out if you get hurt or fall to our tropical heat, so leave now if you gonna be leavin'."

One portly older woman, who was already sweating profusely and sporting beet-red cheeks, opted out. The rest of us fell in line whispering and shuffle-footed behind Rashidi as he continued his commentary.

The scenery was gorgeous, and like nothing I had ever seen. We hiked up a steep, winding path. The trees were tall, with the leaves clustered like a canopy over our heads. At ground level was bush, sparse on the cleared path, but thick up to its edge. As best as I can explain it, bush is whatever grows near the ground: bushes, ferns with giant leaves, weeds, flowers, small trees, and grasses. Rashidi described it all, but I didn't hear most of it. I was concentrating on the challenge of breathing in through my nose and out through my mouth, and on keeping my mind free of him. Of Nick.

The incline winded me, and I scowled at the memories and effect of my recent debauched lifestyle. The burning in my lungs began to feel good; it burned out the bush in me and cleared a path for me to find my way.

We had been hiking for nearly two hours when Rashidi gave us a hydration break and announced that we were nearing the turn-around point, which would be a special treat: a modern ruin. He explained that a bad man, a thief and a thug, had built a beautiful mansion in paradise, named her Annalise, and then left her forsaken and half-complete. No one had ever finished her and the rainforest had moved fast to claim her. Wild horses roamed her halls, colonies of bats filled her eaves, and who knows what lived below her in the depths of her cisterns. We would eat our lunch there, then turn back for the—much easier, he promised—hike down.

When the forest parted to reveal Annalise, we all drew in a breath. She was amazing: tall, austere, and a bit frightening. Our group grew tense. What woman doesn't love going to an open house? And here we were, visiting a mysterious mansion with a romantic history in a tropical rainforest. Ooo la la.

Graceful, flamboyant trees and grand pillars marked the entrance to her gateless drive. On each side of the overgrown road were tropical fruit trees of every description, and the fragrance was pungent, the air drunk with fermenting mangos and ripening guava, subtly undercut by the aroma of bay leaves. It was a surreal orchard, its orphaned fruit unpicked, the air heavy and still, bees and insects the only thing stirring besides our band of turistas. Overhead, the trees' branches met in the middle of the road and were covered in vines with trailing pink flowers. The sun shone through the canopy in narrow beams and lit our dim path.

We climbed up Annalise's ten uneven front steps and entered through what should have been imposing double doors. We came first into a great room with thirty-five-foot ceilings. My skin prickled, each hair standing to salute Annalise. We gazed up in wonder at her intricate tongue-in-groove cypress ceiling with mahogany beams, her improbable stone fireplace here in the tropics.

We explored her three stories, room after room unfolding as we discussed what each was to have been. Balcony floors with no railings jutted from two sides of the house. A giant concrete pool hovered partway out of the ground. How could someone put in so much work, build something magnificent, create such hope, and leave her to rot?

Gradually, ughs replaced the oohs as we discovered that we had to step over horse manure and bat guano in every room. Dead gungalos by the thousands crunched under our feet. One woman put her hand on a wall and ended up with dung between her fingers and gunked into her ostentatious diamond ring, which for some inexplicable reason she'd worn on a rainforest hike. Annalise was not for the faint of heart, and I suppressed my urge to run for a broom. What she could have been was so clear; what she might still be was staggering. I could see it. I could feel it.

And zing, something hit me hard, just coursed through my head and lungs. A cold, hard, lonely place filled with crap. It was like looking in the mirror. No, it was more than that. It was like someone had whispered it in my ear. It felt personal to me that she was abandoned. Even her name resonated inside me: Annalise. Unbelievably, I had a connection on my Treo, and I Googled the origin of the name —Hebrew for grace, favor. For some reason, reading those words hurt me. Annalise and I could both use some grace. An overpowering urge to make things right by myself and by this house rose up in me. I didn't see the irrationality of it; I saw the possibility of mutual redemption. Lost in this feeling, I saved the realtor's name and number from the faded sign by the door into my contacts. It didn't hurt to type it into my memo app, I told myself.

Rashidi's voice broke through my reverie. "Ms. Katie, are you comin' wit' us? It gets dark up here at night, you know."

I laughed and started after the group, excitement bubbling up in me from the inside and spilling over in that forgotten sound of joy. I had energy now and a spring in my step. The group was chattering as we hiked out, but I didn't hear a word. My washing-machine mind was churning again, but instead of Nick, this time it was Annalise spinning through it. It was like she was calling out to me that we were the same, that we could save each other, and my mind answered with a cautious maybe, a tentative "we'll see." I stopped to look back each time she came into view, further and further in the distance.

She was defiantly beautiful and strong, soaring over a sea of green treetops, and behind her, the ocean, which looked like the sky. A view of the world turned upside down. I shivered.

Rashidi dropped back a half-dozen paces from the group and spoke softly to me. "So, you like the house? I see you talkin' to her spirit."

Did this man take me for a crazy person? Or had my lips moved? If I was talking to her, and I was not sure that I had been, I wasn't about to affirm my insanity to a stranger. "Talking to her spirit? What, you mean the spirit of the pooping horse?" I said.

"You make like I crazy, but what that make you? You the one hear the house talkin' to you," he said matter-of-factly. "What she say?"

Instead of answering him, I asked, "Why do you say she's got a spirit? What do you mean, like a ghost?"

Rashidi's speech became more colloquial, his accent thickened, and his eyes sparkled. "Nah, she ain't got no ghost, she is the spirit. She a beautiful woman, abandoned by a man. How does most beautiful womens act when they scorned? She lonely, and she full of spite." He grinned. "She lookin' for a new lover. But most folk too scared of her to take her on. When she don't like someone, she a mean one. She been known to drop a bad man when he come for no good, hit him with a rock from nowhere, or send centipedes to bite him. When she do like somebody, well, some people say she talk to them. Like she talk to you, Ms. Katie."

This made sense to me in a way I could not explain. It wasn't like I was ever going to have to see Rashidi again, so what the heck, I would tell him what I had heard.

"She said we are soulmates." I turned and smiled straight on at him. "In so many words.

He didn't bat an eye. "Yah, I t'ought so. Annalise talk to me sometimes, but today I feel her vibrations, and she talkin' to you. Powerful t'ing. You gonna go back and talk to her again?"

"Ummmm, maybe," I said.

"Let me know if you need a hand. Good to have someone with you what knows the way aroun'."

"I might take you up on that."

He nodded and caught up with the group, exhorting them to "Breathe in the scent of the flowers, ladies, glory in the beauty of the forest, because we are almost back to civilization, and you may never come this way again."

But I knew that I would.

GIVING ME HIVES

Above: Bees dem, at Annaly.

After a few productive fits and starts, work ground to a halt at Annaly. This was not the first time I had experienced a work stoppage out there. Work had stopped before when my container arrived from Miami without my construction supplies. Work ceased temporarily when I fired my first general contractor. Work jammed up when my new workers decided to take a long Fourth of July weekend. In fact, it seemed that there was a lot more work stoppage than work startage up at Annaly.

This time, though, the work stopped because of bees. Yes, bees. Bees as in four very big hives of angry African bees, hives that were affixed overnight to windows, a doorway, and the garage ceiling.

I did what one normally does when infested by raging bees: flipped out. Then I called a specialist. Possibly I am using the word specialist liberally here, but I did call someone who said that for seven hundred dollars he would rid me of my bee problem. How? I figured don't ask/don't tell was the way to go.

Two days later, I dragged my parents, kids, Cowboy, and our new rottweiler Callia (a rescue from the animal shelter) out to Annaly, where we were excited to see that the bee handler had earned his pay. We were bee-free. Being beeless meant work could resume on the house, or at least that it would require a new reason for work to continue not to occur on the house.

While we were there, we were greeted by the welcome wagon— five preteen Cruzan boys toting machetes and BB guns who came up out of the bush to say hello. They entertained us with stories of riding their horses and playing hide-and-seek in the house (which they promised not to do any more), and picking mangoes in the valley I now called my own.

Then an old local guy, whose name I still can't pronounce, rode up on his horse. 'He had toothless gums and well-worn fatigues, and he offered to teach my kids to ride. We agreed that in exchange, he could continue harvesting and selling mangoes from the trees on Annaly's grounds.

I hoped the new neighbors, while not exactly the boy-next-door type, would compensate for the bee trauma. Annaly was testing my mettle, surely, but so far I'd stood my ground.

HI HO SILVER, AWAY!

Jeb, may he rest in peace, was the best dog in the world, or at least on the island of St. Croix. We only had him half the time, as we shared custody with my parents. We hadn't always done that; Jeb used to be solely their dog. He had to start staying with us when my parents were off-island, because he kept leaving Whispering Palms to go on walkabout à la Crocodile Dundee. He would visit neighbors from one end of the island to the other, and eventually someone would drop him at the vet, who was quite adamant that the walkabouts must stop. Cruzans are not great drivers, and Jeb preferred to travel down the center of the roadways.

At our house, Jeb became Cowboy's love object. Cowboy, at one year of age and a mere shadow of his future self, already outweighed Jeb by thirty pounds. It was a serious case of tough love. Imagine Cowboy standing at the back door of the house when he would spy Jeb standing fifteen feet away. With one leap, Cowboy would land on

Jeb for the Power Hump, a move reminiscent of Tonto mounting his horse from the back by vaulting on. Cowboy would crush Jeb to the floor and they would skid another five feet together and slam into the far wall. Even the impact would not dislodge Cowboy. No wonder Jeb went on walkabout.

Jeb, if he could have talked, would have told you how very happy he was every time my parents came back to St. Croix and rescued him from Cowboy. I hope his sudden and inexplicable death at the age of eight was in no part caused by Cowboy's love.

We miss that dog, all of us do, especially Cowboy.

RATS, AND I DON'T MEAN DARN.

Dear Diary,

The creatures of the field should remain in the field, and not come into my house. Since we moved in (a whole two weeks ago), I have had a problem with rats and mice at Annaly. Well, bats, geckos, frogs, gungalos, and centipedes, too, but for now, I'll stick to the rodent issue.

The rats are brazen. If food is left on a counter, they will come out and t'ief it {Yo, non-Cruzans, that means steal it.} right in front of me. I knew we had rats hiding in the chimney because I'd seen one scamper up there to safety. I bought poisons, traps, and sticky paper, but was too squeamish to use them. Hold that thought.

While I may consider myself the butt-kicking Amazon of the Cruzan rainforest, even I am not about to spend the night *alone* in Wuthering Heights without a generator or any flashlights. So one night when I had exactly this issue, a perfect storm of unpreparedness if you will, Sasha, Valerie, and baby Marcia came over.

Sasha and Valerie are both bahn'yah{Born here.} Cruzans, so I thought they could help me with my rat issues, but they were drinking red wine. Red wine and rat traps don't mix. So we sat up chatting until the wee hours in the great room under the clothesline I had rigged around the four-story-high scaffolding since the drier wasn't working yet. The laundry blew like flags in the night breeze from the open windows.

We all played slumber party in the master bedroom, Marcia in her playpen, the three of us grown-ups sardined in the king-size bed. About five a.m., I heard a thrum like a guitar chord. I roused Valerie. "Do you hear that? It sounds like something is playing with Clark's guitar."

Valerie said, "No, that's a mouse in the refrigerator something-or-other."

How the heck she knew that, lying somewhat drunk in a bed all the way across the big echo-y house, is beyond me. I went to look. Sure enough, she was right. Great.

I left Sasha and Marcia asleep and made Valerie come with me to the kitchen. I briefly considered going outside to get the dogs—Cowboy, Callia, and my new baby German shepherd, Little Bear—but I realized this was a job for a cat. I posted Juliet {Our new Cruzan kitty.} at the top of the pantry, and we pulled the back top panel off the fridge to let the rodent free while she mewled in interest. We congratulated each other and returned to bed, assuming Juliet would be successful. But one should never assume, right?

The next night, after we had returned from a "lovely" dinner at Blue Moon on the West End during which Clark had ugly mood swings and Susanne fell asleep, I straightened up the kitchen. I went to the pantry to put up a box of Cheez-Its, and found myself face-to-face with the granddaddy of all bush rats. I handled this well, thank you very much: I screamed my lungs out. Then, I took Juliet back into the kitchen for a second try. I put her up top, grabbed a box of Kraft Shells & Cheese, and shooed the rat out. Juliet didn't move. I threw the macaroni box. It stunned the rat in midair, and I whacked it again with a box of Duncan Hines brownie mix when it hit the ground.

"El raton es muerto!" I yelled. I don't normally speak Spanish and have no idea where this came from.

My joy was short-lived; I had to clean up the mess, and boy was I nauseous at this point. Plus I had remembered that where there's one rat, there's a rat family. In the chimney, no less. Project Burn 'Em Out would commence that weekend if the cats didn't start making an impact {After the addition of one more cat (Tiger), the felines stepped up to the plate and the rodents went back to the fields—no need for fires.}.

BAD MAN DEM

Adapted excerpt from the novel *Leaving Annalise*, sequel to *Saving Grace*:

It started with the chows. {This excerpt is a perfect example of a fictional story ripped from our real life.}

"Kate," Ms. Ruthie called through the open kitchen window to me from the driveway. She always called me Kate, never Katie. "Come. There's some big dogs outside."

On St. Marcos, one did not say, "Come here, please," one simply commanded, "Come." It sounded rude to those from off-island at first, but you quickly got used to it. I appreciated the economy of expression.

Looking out the kitchen window, I saw a couple of large chows sniffing around the empty bowls we had fed our dogs from earlier. Ours as in mine, Annalise's, and Ruthie's.

Now that she had my attention, Ruthie continued. "I don't like them dogs. Chows mean. They could hurt Taylor bad. They could hurt any of us." Ruthie was the temporary nanny to Taylor, the toddler visiting for the summer with his Uncle Nick. The Nick I was coming to think of as my Nick, here on the island where I had escaped his memory, only to have the real Nick show up and reclaim me a year later. I hadn't resisted nearly as hard as I had planned.

"Where'd they come from? I've never noticed them before," I replied.

She chuptzed. "Those boys growing ganja across the road near the old Rasta shanty. They bring the dogs dem this week. Guard dogs."

This took me by surprise, but I didn't question her, as it made perfect sense.

That night I said, "Nick, you realize this is your fault?"

"How is it my fault?" he asked as he snuggled in tight behind me in bed.

"My life had no crossover with the criminal element until I met you. Now I have the son of a drug dealer living in the house, and our neighbors have set up a marijuana production facility across the road." Taylor's father was serving time in a Texas prison for selling drugs. Nice.

"Believe me, I'd like to send all the criminals back to wherever they came from," he said. Then he bit the back of my neck in exactly the right way to end the conversation.

Over the next two days, the chows visited more frequently, agitating our six dogs: no mayhem, just growls and posturing.

On the third day, Ms. Ruthie called out to me from the driveway again. "Come. Dogs dem harassing Taylor." And in this case, the tone of her "come" said "urgent, come quickly."

Outside, Ruthie pointed to the end of the driveway. The pack of big chows stood with their tails erect and the dogs were clustered in front of them, all of them growling. Taylor sat on the ground behind our dogs, playing with one of his trucks and talking earnestly to my German shepherd, Oso. I couldn't understand anything he said, but Oso usually seemed to speak his language. Today the chows had Oso's full attention.

As the danger to Taylor dawned on me, I felt an unexpected rage build in me. I was a beast. I wanted to rush those chows and kill them with my bare hands.

"Shoo!" I yelled, to little effect. I was an ineffective beast.

Something clanged to the ground behind me, a gift from another angry beast. "Thanks, Annalise," I said. I grabbed the heavy shovel that had appeared where none had been before.

I advanced on the dogs with my weapon raised, yelling in my deepest voice, "Get out of here! Go! Go now!" The chows backed away, but in no hurry. They seemed more annoyed than scared.

Then the largest chow snarled and lunged at me. Oso met its lunge in a blur of tan and black fur and gnashing teeth. I scooped up Taylor, who was clutching his truck in a death grip. I ran for the house with Ruthie on my heels. All the dogs joined Oso in a deafening melee. Nick pounded into the kitchen.

"What is it?" he asked.

"Our dogs, the chows, a fight," I panted.

Nick sprinted outside, screaming at the dogs, but by the time he got there, the chows had run back toward the shanty. Our dogs stalked around on stiff legs, itching for more of a fight. After a few minutes, they calmed down and licked their wounds. None of them had sustained grave injuries. Oso was hurt the worst.

"Good dog, Oso," I said, and stroked his head as he followed Nick into the bathroom for some minor TLC.

In the quiet that followed, Taylor resumed his game on the kitchen floor, singing to himself. The blood rushed out of my head and I had to sit on a stool and press my face against the cool granite countertop.

Ms. Ruthie placed an icy cold rag on the side of my face. *Angel.*

Nick and Oso rejoined us. I sat up and moved the cold cloth to my forehead. Nick smoothed the back of my disheveled hair. We discussed options.

"Should we call the police?" Nick asked.

I'd been on-island long enough to know this was a dangerous idea. "I'm afraid it wouldn't be too hard for them to figure out who tattled on them, and we would be sitting ducks up here if they decided to retaliate. Maybe the animal shelter would pick them up?"

Nick mulled this over. "*If* they could catch them. And, following your line of reasoning, that might be too obviously linked to us as well." He snapped his fingers. "But what if we could borrow a few of the shelter's cages and trap the dogs here?" He motioned out the window. "They look like they're starving. If we baited the traps, maybe with hot dogs or bacon or something, they'd be in there in a flash. And then we could take them down to the shelter ourselves, one at a time. As far as the bad guys would know, the dogs would simply be disappearing, one by one, with no explanation, and they'd probably think they ran off or died."

Ms. Ruthie and I liked that idea, so we went with it. It only took five days and five trips to the animal shelter to get rid of the dogs. The chows showed surprising docility once caged, but I still let Nick handle all the close work.

Our plan had an unexpected benefit: the drug farmers disappeared, too. Losing their dogs seemed to make them skittish. We high-fived and resumed normal operations. I found a yellow sticky on the mirror that night: "Smile, beautiful. We busted up a drug farm together. How amazing is that?" I smiled.

But that night, we heard mournful howling and distressed barking from the direction of the farm.

"I need to check that out," Nick decided. He put on black jeans and a long-sleeved black shirt, grabbed a flashlight and the machete. "If I'm not back in an hour, call Rashidi," he instructed me.

"This seems like a crummy idea, Nick."

He grinned at me and walked backwards toward the door, saying in his best St. Marcos accent, "Me ain't 'fraid of dem atall," and disappeared into the night.

Sitting on the front steps, I watched his flashlight bob along in the distant bush. The barking rose to a fever pitch, and then abruptly stopped. This was nerve-wracking. I bit my lip. Only thirty-five minutes had passed. Should I call Rashidi? I leaned against the porch column with my face against its cool stones. No, I would stick to the plan. I hated being the damsel left behind.

Nick reappeared at forty-seven minutes. I didn't see him until he was almost to the house. He waved to me, but headed straight to the garage. I jumped up and loped after him. When I reached the garage, he was scooping dog food into bags and filling gallon jugs with water.

He turned to me, his face red and fierce. "Those assholes left two dogs up there chained to trees to guard the bathtubs they were using as marijuana pots. The dogs are nothing but spinal columns, twig legs, and giant heads, and they have scuba weights strapped to their collars. The bastards took out all their plants, but they left the dogs to die."

My stomach clenched. "Oh my God, that's awful."

"I didn't get too near them in case they still had the energy to attack. I'm going to take them some food and water."

"Why don't you set them free? Those poor dogs."

"I don't want to give the assholes any reason to feel threatened. I'd like to leave the dogs in place for a few more days, in case they come back. I can take supplies out there every night. If the farmers don't come back, I'll cut the dogs loose."

He was already striding off with his arms full. "I'm coming with you!" I said.

"No, stay here with Taylor. Everything's OK. I'll be back soon."

I stayed, growing angrier about the dogs by the second. Nick returned faster this time. The dogs had been so eager for the water and food that they overcame their distrust of him and slunk forward on their bellies to accept it.

Each night for three more nights, he repeated his mission. We saw no sign of the thugs. On the fourth night, he took bolt cutters and set the dogs free. One of them rocketed away into the night. The other followed Nick back to our house.

"He's so skinny!" I said.

"He's put on several pounds in the last few days. You should have seen him before," Nick replied.

"His head looks huge on his skeleton body. What kind of dog is he supposed to be?"

"He's a pit bull cross. I call him Big Head." He patted said head. His voice had taken on a paternal tone.

Uh oh. "Nick, you know we can't keep this dog. He's been abused, he's sick—we can't trust him around Taylor."

Nick cast his eyes down. "I know. I just feel so bad for him."

I did, too, but it was clear what needed to be done. Big Head joined the chows at the shelter the next day. Now there were no predators—human or canine—to contend with across the street.

MÉNAGE À TORTOISE

Above: Count 'em: One, two, t'ree turtles.

One of the most awesome parts of living in the islands is getting out on the water. Owning a boat? A pain in the rear. Having friends with boats? Perfect. Eric and I joined our friends for a boat ride one Sunday after we were engaged, and off in the distance as we passed Judith's Fancy on the north shore, we saw a floater. None of us could decide what it was. A log? A lost canoe?

We pulled closer. Nope, not a log or canoe. Three turtles, as in ménage à tortoise. This gives love a bad name, but it made for a hell of a picture.

CHESTER

One week, for one whole glorious week, we had an actual pig up at Annaly. An unplanned pig. An unplanned pig is kind of like an unplanned pregnancy. It's big and undeniable, and it's totally undignified. Kind of like our lives. The pig showed up as an evictee from the refinery's housing camp, in need of a home. We moved him in, named him Chester, and we loved him.

Chester weighed about forty-five pounds, or approximately the same as our smallest guard mutt, Jake the Snake. Jake was actually a cockermation, not a snake {Female Dalmatian mother, male cocker spaniel father. A fantabulous mix!}. He got his name from Jake Plummer, the erstwhile quarterback of the Arizona Cardinals. I thought maybe Chester and Jake could hang, be pals, be running buddies.

Jake thought not. Jake may have shunned Chester, but Callia, our rottweiler, took an instant liking to him. Kind of in the way she liked porterhouse steak.

"Leave him alone, Callia," I commanded, over and over, as Callia chased Chester and nipped at the back of his neck.

I participated in my first-ever triathlon that weekend. Clark and Susanne showed up with posters that read, "Go Mom," in tiny letters. It wasn't their fault it was hardly legible—the words just wouldn't fit around their giant drawing of Chester, bright white with gorgeous black spots.

Chester spent a happy week eating our table scraps. Since we had no garbage disposal, Chester's popularity rating soared, as far as I was concerned. I hated composting. Pig feeding, though? I could do that. He let me scratch his rough back and smooth down his wiry hair while he snorted and ate.

On day seven of our Chester era, I went out to feed the dogs, who now numbered six—along with Jake, Eric had brought his boxer Layla and his German shepherd Karma. Yes, oh my. For six days, Chester had trotted behind the dogs, eager to be in on any eating opportunity. For six days, I had giggled at his cloppety steps and his farty snorts that were forced out each time a hoof hit the ground.

Today, no Chester.

"Chester? Here, piggy piggy piggy. Come on, Chester," I called, unperturbed at first. Maybe he was scavenging for mangoes or soursop. He'd probably show up with a buzz from the fermented fruit.

No Chester.

"Eric, I can't find Chester," I called into the house.

A few moments later, Eric emerged from the house dressed for work. We exchanged a smooch.

"Chester hasn't shown up," I explained. "I was about to look for him."

"I'm sorry, babe," he said. "Do you need my help?"

"No, go on to work. I'll look for him after I take the kids to school."

"I'll take the kids. No need for you to make a trip out."

"Thanks, love."

I went back into the house to gather the children. Five minutes later I had them in Eric's little Toyota truck, Clark holding a loaded toothbrush in one hand and a glass of water in the other. "Use that thing," I said, pointing at the toothbrush.

Clark nodded. I blew a kiss. And they were off.

Dread began to constrict my chest and my throat. To put off the hunt for Chester, I did my normal morning routine, loading the dishwasher, gathering laundry, and booting up my computer for work. The view from my office over Mango Valley and into the ruins of an old sugar mill beat Eric's view over the back parking lot of a 500,000-barrel-per-day oil refinery.

Finally, I could avoid the issue no longer. I put on my hiking boots and some jeans. I loaded a small bucket with breakfast scraps. I called to Cowboy and set off to find our pig. Only fifteen minutes later, my fears were confirmed. I saw the small white mound, crumpled underneath one of the big mango trees behind the house.

"Oh, Chester," I said as I knelt beside him.

Eric loved pigs, had always wanted a pig. I was pretty fond of pigs myself and spent many happy times feeding them at my grandparents' farm in Stephenville, Texas, years ago. I was especially fond of this pig, though. How quickly love sneaks up on you.

I placed my hand on his side. He was cold and firm. I combed over his body, looking for a clue to the cause of death. The only thing out of the ordinary was a pair of puncture marks in his back. I didn't have Callia with me to measure the span between her canines, but I didn't really want that level of certainty. An image formed in my mind of her dragging Chester to the ground and breaking his back with the weight of her body. I forced the image out. If she had killed him, why had she left him alone? Why hadn't she, well, *eaten* him?

I used the top of my right forearm to wipe away my tears and stood up. I placed the bucket near Chester's head and walked back into the house. Knowing how he died wouldn't bring the cheery little pig back.

Later, we buried him under his favorite mango tree. Chester would always have a place at Annaly, in paradise.

EVERY DOG HAS ITS DAY.

This is a story about Layla, sweet Layla the boxer who has the misfortune to look like Gollum from *Lord of the Rings*. It's the story of how she returned to us from the dead.

When Layla moved into Annaly, she was only about six months old. St. Croix, unfortunately, has an underground dogfighting community. As a female boxer, she was a sought-after sort of dog on the island—a young bitch who could mother fighting pups. We came home one day to discover she was gone, had simply vanished. We put fliers up all over the island offering a reward for her return, but we had no luck. After a few weeks, we sadly accepted the reality that she would not ever be coming back.

Four months later, we got a call from the animal shelter. "I think someone brought in your female boxer, that one from your flier last summer, but we can't be sure. She's pretty far gone, and we're planning to put her down. Do you want to come in and see her before we do?"

Did we?!? Eric and I jumped in my big Chevy Silverado truck and practically flew over the giant tire-eating potholes on our way down out of the rainforest and into town. When we came to an abrupt, breathless halt twenty minutes later, Eric turned to me.

"Why don't you wait in the car, just in case?" He cupped my cheek in his hand.

"Yes," I said. The woman from the shelter had warned us that Layla—if this was Layla—was not only barely recognizable, but that her skin was practically hairless and weeping with open sores. Still, I felt weak for staying behind.

Eric went off to view the dog. I could see him from the back. He crouched in front of a mobile kennel, reached out his hand, and I saw a long pink tongue, but could make out nothing else in the dark opening where the dog lay. Then Eric turned back toward me and I saw the tears on his face.

It was Layla. I got out of the car, crying and feeling nauseous. I walked over and stood beside him. I would not have recognized her. Eric barely had. But she recognized him, and with what little strength she had remaining, she had lifted her head, whimpered, and reached for him with her funny, oversized tongue that looked like the vintage Rolling Stones posters.

Thirty minutes later, we had transported Layla to our veterinarian against the advice of the shelter. Layla, we were now told, had mange, an easily treated condition that she was born with, unbeknownst to us, because it doesn't become symptomatic until a dog begins to mature. We surmised that it had raged out of control until she had been dumped in the road in the center of the island and left for dead. Some goodhearted soul had braved her oozing sores to bring her to the shelter, even knowing it might be hopeless for her. We decided to let our vet make the call. If he thought he could save her, we would let him try.

Dr. Hess did believe he could, and he did save her.

It took many weeks of intensive treatment at his clinic to get her well enough to come home. We visited her daily and tried not to look at the receipts when they ran our credit card. Layla had never wowed us with her beauty, but now she was scary ugly, a skinny, hairless, pink-skinned waif who still had silver-dollar-sized open wounds when we brought her home six weeks later.

When the time came to move to the states, Layla flew ahead to live with Eric's oldest daughter in Auburn. But Layla was soon kicked out of Marie's apartment complex, and she moved to Texas, where she has lived with us ever since.

Layla lives the good life now. She is Cowboy's devoted partner and companion, and the two of them behave like an old married couple. She hasn't gotten much prettier, and she is very, very afraid of men, especially men with dark skin. But she has for the most part overcome four months of hell and two months of pain to become a loving and normal dog.

Layla. Survivor of violent kidnapping, abuse, and neglect. Left for dead. Our muscley little protector who likes you to whisper sweet nothings into her oversized ears as you pet them.

I think there is a special place in hell for people who hurt children and animals, and I hope her abusers find their way to it. And I also believe there is a place in heaven for people who give their time and love to those who can't take care of themselves. We will always be grateful to the kind person who rescued Layla, all those years ago.

THE GIMPY CHICKEN

When Eric and I left St. Croix, we not only had a big jumbie house to sell and six dogs and two cats in need of homes, but a chain of GNC stores and triathlon shops on two islands to deal with, too. Alas, try as we might, the stores would not be sold; they met their fate in bankruptcy proceedings a year later. In the here-and-now that was then, we spent two miserable rainy weekends laying the stores on St. Thomas to rest.

The first weekend, we took the ferry over. Actually, I'm being generous and disingenuous in calling it the ferry, because it never went by any other name at our house than the Vomit Comet. And indeed, vomit I did. Vomit, vomit, and more vomit. Tiny Susanne ended up asleep alone inside the ferry, while Eric held me around the waist to keep me from going overboard along with my lunch.

The second weekend, you couldn't have gotten me on the Vomit Comet if you dragged me behind a Wild West stagecoach. And if you had been able to get me on, Eric would have dragged me back off again. The experience hadn't exactly lit him up with happy, either. Instead, we took the seaplane.

The seaplane takes off from the bay in Christiansted and lands in the bay of Charlotte Amalie. It's a fun experience, if you block out the fact that Eric's father lost an eye, a leg, and nearly his life in a seaplane crash during takeoff from Christiansted less than twenty years before. I blocked it out. The choice between death and two hours barfing aboard the Vomit Comet was an easy one.

For three days we disassembled and fire-sold the remains of the St. Thomas stores. It was a grim affair. We were exhausted and heart-broken, but we thanked God for our time together, anyway. And we cried a little. It could have gone so differently. Less greed and theft, more oversight, fewer customers shaving off pennies in the short run by shopping online, and the stores might have made it.

The time came to depart Charlotte Amalie to go back to St. Croix. We sat pressed together on a bench in the open-air departure lounge, our heads back against the wall, our fingers entwined. Gradually, I became aware of a new entrant to the lounge. It was a scraggly, limping chicken, begging for food, traveler by traveler. His feathers were oily, the tuft on his head askew. He fit in well, even as he was so decidedly odd.

"Check out the gimpy chicken," I said to Eric.

The chicken hobbled over to the next passenger and peered up at him through a half-closed eye with his head cocked. No success.

"I see him," Eric said, chuckling.

The chicken scratched the ground and pecked at nothing, then tried his gambit on the next person. The little old West Indian lady dropped him a spoonful of rice and peas from her Styrofoam container. He gobbled it up, then she shooed him away. He retreated six inches, then continued his march down the row of people.

I put on my really bad Cruzan accent. "Feed a hungry chicken, meh son. Put food in de mouts of me chirrun dem."

Eric shook his head at my accent. A lifelong Cruzan, his accent was real, although most of the time he yanked like a continental. "Isn't it appropriate, as we are here closing these stores that failed in part because of the culture of these islands—everybody thinking they're owed something, entitled to be given something by someone else—that the chicken is here looking for a handout, too?"

The chicken finished working the line and disappeared around the corner.

"I'll bet when he went around the corner, he took off that fake leg, combed his feathers, and walked off home, hale and hearty. The end of his shift," I said.

And we laughed and then laughed some more, a sad sound that turned into something like real happiness as it went on, and we saluted the little bird as we walked to our plane and left our bitterness mostly behind.

A LOT LIKE CANNIBALS

Adapted excerpt from the novel *Leaving Annalise (Katie #2)*:

It was time to go. Nick and I developed a "this and no more" final work list for Annalise. We retained a real estate agent. We printed fliers and an ad for an estate sale, and Nick ran them into town. I packed the things we would take and laid out the things that we would sell. I tried to book travel off-island, but the airport remained closed. Ten days before, a Category 4 hurricane had damaged the airport, although it hadn't so much as nicked Annalise's fortress.

I emailed Nick from my phone about the travel roadblock—or airblock, rather—but I stayed calm. We knew that getting back to Texas was not going to be simple. "We may need to find a boat ride out of here. The storm damaged the terminal, and American won't resume flights until it's repaired, which could be months."

"We can try to hire a boat captain here," Nick emailed back.

I was feeding the dogs while I emailed him, and I noticed something seemed off. I did a head count. Our big rottweiler wasn't there. She didn't often miss a meal.

I sent Nick a text. "Have you seen Sheila? She didn't come in for food."

"Nope. Not since yesterday. Smile, Katie: Ole Sheila must have a boyfriend somewhere."

I smiled.

I set back to work. We knew our plan was ambitious. We had one more day to prepare for the estate sale, then the sale day itself. On the very next day, we would leave St. Marcos, somehow, any way we could. Nick wanted me to go back to the states with him so we could raise his orphaned nephew, Taylor, who was waiting for us in Corpus Christi with Nick's parents. It was the right thing to do. It was the only thing to do. Wasn't it?

Later, neither Nick nor I could find any boat captains on St. Marcos willing to leave their homes and families. In the states, people jump at the chance to make extra money. There, everyone was aghast at the idea of working during the post-hurricane bonus holiday.

I tried some of the smaller airlines that flew from island to island. The damaged terminal might not have affected them as much as it had the major airlines. And it really didn't matter where we flew to, as long as we could eventually get somewhere to catch a connecting flight to the states. By the third airline, I had found our ride. LIAT, an airline locals describe as "Leave Islands Any Time," would be doing just that, starting the next day. I booked us on a flight to Aruba with Oso where we could make connections to the states. As I hung up, the agent said, "Mind your dog don't weigh no more than a hunner pound with he kennel." We hung up.

"All set," I called from the kitchen to Nick in the garage. "You don't think Oso and his kennel are over one hundred pounds, do you?"

Nick walked into the kitchen. "About one-fifteen, I'd say. Why?"

My heart sunk from diaphragm to belly-button level. Much further and it was going to drop out in my lap. "Oh, no! He's over the weight limit to fly."

Nick shook his head. "No way we're leaving Oso. Don't worry about it. I'll handle this one."

"Really?" I asked, grateful to cross one thing off my daunting to-do list.

"No problem," he said, and swatted my behind. I swatted his back.

All the next day we focused on preparing for our sale. It boggled my mind how much I had accumulated on St. Marcos in just over a year. Everything we sold left one less thing to ship to the states or to "walk off" (be carried away by a thief) from Annalise. Whatever we didn't sell, we would leave with the house for the buyer to deal with —when we found one.

Really, we were worried less about all of that and more about Sheila. Out of our six dogs, Oso was the only pet, but we loved the rest of the pack, too, and took good care of them. Oso would come to the states with us, though. The others would stay to guard Annalise. I ran Oso into the vet for a travel clearance check, since the airlines would not transport him into the continental U.S. without a letter testifying to his good health. While I was there, I put up a lost-dog notice for Sheila with my friend Ava's phone number on it. She would house-sit Annalise and care for the remaining dogs until Annalise sold.

We had announced in the *St. Marcos Daily Source* that our sale would begin at eight in the morning. Cars lined up at our gate at seven and started honking. We knew the people of St. Marcos loved nothing more than a good estate sale, but this was too much. We ignored them as we did our last-minute preparations and slammed down some local King's coffee.

It was another typically beautiful day, and I steeled myself for it. I was leaving Annalise of my own volition, but not without great sadness. The sight of my things spread out on the driveway made our departure feel real. I hated parting with the baby toys and high chair that I'd bought for Taylor just four months ago at someone else's estate sale. Nick stepped on a squeaky stuffed animal just then and let out a yelp. I laughed, because what else could I do?

At 7:45, we took pity on the early birds and opened the gate, ignoring their comments and long drawn-out chuptzes. The posturing and haggling began at once. I did not enjoy this, but here Nick was my polar opposite. So I played Wal-Mart greeter and handled merchandise security while Nick played the used car salesman.

"How much you want for the pitcher, meh son?" a steely-haired West Indian man asked.

"Fifty," Nick said firmly.

"Whaaaaat?" More chuptzing. "I give you thirty, and you still be taking food out the mouths of me children dem."

"Forty-five," Nick responded.

Muttering, mild cursing, more chuptzing. "You thiefing me and no lie. I give you thirty-five, and that's as high as I go."

"Forty, and that's the final price." Nick said, and turned to walk away to another customer. As the old gentleman nodded and picked up the framed print, Nick called out to me, "Forty for this picture, Katie," and I hustled over to take the money and be sure that art was all that he loaded into the car.

As I rang him out, I realized things weren't going so well with Nick and the next customer. I looked up and my heart sank. The customer was an electrician that Junior—the contractor I'd fired long ago—had brought in to work on the house; the same electrician who did such a poor job that we had refused to pay his full bill. Call me crazy, but when you turn on the light, it shouldn't run the garbage disposal, too. He was now giving Nick a bit of a rash, proclaiming for all within earshot to hear that we were leaving the island without paying him the rest of the money we owed him. But he wasn't able to maintain the threat for long.

The growl that emanated from Oso's throat was so menacing, I was afraid of him myself. He'd stepped into Sheila's alpha dog role without hesitation. The electrician made haste to depart, with Oso as his escort.

"Good dog, Oso," I said as he trotted back to me. I praised and petted him, to his delight and the jealous consternation of his canine companions.

The sale went on for hours, with friends and acquaintances showing up off and on during the morning. By midday it had become an impromptu pool party, and we finally shut the gate and counted our money.

"Eighteen thousand dollars. Not bad at all," I said.

"That's great! I expected half that," Nick replied.

"How about we use our guests to help us clean out the refrigerator?" I suggested.

"You're good-looking and you're smart, too," he said, which I took for a yes.

We carried a smorgasbord down to the pool. Some of the people who had celebrated our wedding with us in this same place a month before were now gathered here again. It was bittersweet.

Ms. Ruthie showed up to say goodbye. "You tell that boy I love him," she said sternly, and turned away to hide the sadness on her face. She embraced both of us and marched back to her car in her dignified way. I swallowed the huge lump in my throat.

"Ms. Katie," called out one of the children, "What's wrong with that big dog over there?"

Nick and I turned and ran to where the child was pointing. Poor Sheila was staggering around the yard with her face and neck so swollen that they squeezed her eyes shut.

Our neighbor Paul came up behind us. "Looks like your dog got into a swarm of those African bees. That happened to one of our dogs, too. He lived for a few days, but he didn't make it."

I remembered the giant hives that had appeared overnight on Annalise and had cost a pretty penny to have removed. The rainforest found the weakness in everyone, sooner or later. Nick helped Sheila lie down in the soft dirt by the driveway. He shooed the other dogs away. "I don't think Sheila's going to be with us much longer either."

We stroked Sheila behind her ears and offered her some water, but she wouldn't take it. Our mood grew somber and it spread to our friends, who packed up and began to take their leave. The goodbyes felt anticlimactic and mechanical, but I did my best, and then sat back down with Sheila.

I felt a chill and shivered. Sometimes I forgot what a tough place St. Marcos could be. But it wasn't that recognition that made me tremble; it was the contrast between how safe we had all felt up at Annalise until now and the timing of this tragedy with Sheila as we left. I didn't know what to make of it.

"She's stopped breathing," Nick said. "Looks like the old girl wanted to come home and say goodbye."

We put our foreheads together and breathed deeply. After a few moments of silence, we carried Sheila away from the house and found a good resting spot for her under a shady mango tree. We covered her body with branches and returned slowly to the house, walking with our hands clasped white-knuckled, each lost in our thoughts.

Over the next few hours, I cleaned up the aftermath from our estate sale to the sounds of the Dixie Chicks' mournful album *Home*. I played it over and over like a wake for Sheila, like a wake for our life here. It was not the only mournful element in my day. Annalise felt like a teenage girl with her sulk on.

"I'm going to miss you, Annalise. I'm really, really sorry about this," I said aloud.

The house remained still, silent, and morose. Well, if she was going to pout, there was nothing I could do about it. *You're doing the right thing*, I reminded myself for the zillionth time.

Nick walked in from the garage and some of the fog of melancholy lifted.

"Hi, love. Did you feed the dogs yet?" I asked.

"Not yet," he replied.

"I'll go," I said. "I want to do it one more time." I walked toward the side door.

"Wait." Nick's tone stopped me short. "Don't go outside yet."

"What's outside, Nick?" I asked.

"Trust me. It's nothing, and I'll take care of it."

"Which is it: nothing, or something you'll take care of?"

Nick looked back and forth from me to the door—one Scylla and the other Charybdis—and spoke. "The dogs found Sheila."

"What do you mean, 'found her?'" I probed.

"Well, the dogs think they're in the Fiji Islands instead of the West Indies."

It took me a moment, but when understanding dawned, it dawned like a blinding strobe light. "They're eating Sheila?" My lunch of turkey and Swiss sandwich churned with the mango in my stomach.

"Past tense. She's pretty far gone. I'm sorry, Katie."

I knew from experience that the prickly feeling in my face meant the pale between my freckles had turned to pasty. I sank onto a barstool and put my head in my hands. Nick sat beside me. We held onto each other for several quiet moments.

"Are you going to bury her?" I asked into his chest.

"We sold the shovel this morning," he replied.

He was right. "Five dollah? That's criminal," the man who bought it had said as he fished the money out of his wallet.

For some reason, that's what brought on my tears. "But we can't just leave her there," I protested, chagrined to hear the tremor in my voice. More softly, I added, "Or what's left of her."

"I'll cover her up so nothing else can get at her," Nick promised as he stroked my hair.

Mollified, I wiped my eyes and nodded. Nick went out to deal with Sheila and the cannibals. Annalise remained still and quiet. *Some help you are,* I thought.

I fought against the mental image of Oso and the other dogs over Sheila's body; it was too horrifying. Sheila had mothered Oso when I first got him. I flinched as I heard a thud and a crack outside. Nick must have dropped something over Sheila; rocks or bricks, maybe.

I tried to be rational: these were island dogs, and it wasn't as if they'd killed her to eat her. She just happened to be available. But no matter how I tried to spin it for myself, at the end of the day, they ate their friend.

What an unsettling way to end our time on St. Marcos.

PART TWO: NORTHERN MIGRATION

IT'S DE ISLANS, MON

It came time to move to Houston, and Cowboy and his kennel, it turned out, were over the weight limit to fly on the only large commercial plane leaving the island. To Clark and Susanne's horror, we started to search for a new island home for Cowboy. Our search was fruitless, though, and when it became clear that this was not going to be the solution, we put Cowboy on a diet.

Eric felt so bad about starving him that he put all six dogs on a diet, but that plan backfired. Cowboy ate as much as he wanted out of the other dogs' bowls before he let them have any. He didn't lose any weight, but all the rest of the dogs got a little gaunt.

In addition to dieting and adoption, we looked into different transportation options. There weren't many viable alternatives for either dogs or people, and those that we did find, like the private plane that would transport him to the mainland where he could hop a bus or train, were prohibitively expensive. Clark, Susanne, and I finally had to leave for Houston; Eric and Cowboy stayed on the island.

A few months later, it was time for Eric to leave, too. He called to tell us that while he was going to try his best, Cowboy was still too big to fly, although Karma would sail through baggage with no problems. Layla was already in the states with Marie. Little Bear had died when he was less than a year old, the victim of a second round of African bee stings, to which he was highly allergic. Callia had happily moved in with a good friend of ours. We had a contingency plan for Cowboy, if he couldn't make it: he could continue guarding Annaly with Jake for the house sitters while we kept looking for an adoptive family.

The day before his departure, Eric visited the airport and certain key airport and airline officials. He toted a wallet full of hundred-dollar bills, and left those he visited more well-off than he found them. Hey, remember, it's de islands, mon. People were shockingly more eager to transport Cowboy after that visit, but Eric still had to make it through the ticket agent and the baggage handlers the next day.

With his kennel, Cowboy weighed in at a whopping 135 pounds. The weight limit was 100. There was absolutely no pretending the scale was wrong, and it was unlikely that someone would conclude, "Oh, he's close enough, just send him through!" Cowboy was thirty-five percent over the weight limit. Even a casual heft of the corner of his kennel made it obvious that there was way too much dog in there.

Eric brought his wallet to the ticket counter and set some of its contents on top of the kennel when it was placed on the scale. Cowboy lost a few pounds in that transaction, Eric reclaimed his wallet, and Cowboy sailed through to baggage, "No problem, mon."

But in the baggage area, things went awry.

"No way, mon, dis dog not weigh no hunner pounds!" Eric heard the baggage handler shout. "Dis not my jawb to lift he."

In vain, Eric begged, pleaded, explained, and bribed. Not a single person was swayed by his description of his sobbing, brokenhearted children.

"Was de problem ovuh hee-yah?" another baggage handler inquired.

Eric turned towards a familiar voice and looked into the face of a schoolmate from his St. Dunstan's days. Eric hailed him up, and they reminisced about old times for a few moments. Then Eric launched into the tale of woe with his old chum. And just like that, Cowboy made it onto the plane. When Eric told us the news, Clark actually cried.

Eric, Cowboy, and Karma arrived well after midnight that night in Houston. Cowboy did not seem to lose any weight on the trip, nor did he display an appropriate amount of gratitude to Eric. As a new step-dad, though, Eric had forever secured his place in the hearts of Cowboy's fan club.

THE BIRD MAN

Not everything our beloveds do makes sense. Hello, remember Eric's frog obsession? And so it is that my husband has been a fan of the Arizona Cardinals for over forty years. How, one would rightly ask, could something like this happen to a young boy from the Virgin Islands? Some say he was born the patron saint of lost causes, but it's actually much simpler than that: he was brainwashed.

Eric spent a lot of time in his earliest years with his Hungarian grandmother, who married an Italian named Cardinale. The family changed their name to Cardinal. They embraced their name and decorated their home with cardinals. Young Eric began his life-long obsession with football surrounded by cardinals, at the knee of a Cardinal. He turned on the TV and saw the Cardinals in their beautiful scarlet uniforms, and could have drawn no other conclusion than the one he did—the Cardinals were HIS team!

He has stood by them in bad times and in more bad times. He has borne ridicule most men could scarce endure. Through it all, he has held his head high. The highlight of 2006 was our trip to Phoenix for the National Petrochemical and Refiners Association's annual meeting, because we got to go to Eric's first home Cardinals game—in their new stadium, no less. They lost, of course, to the Kansas City

Chiefs. One thing that we're never at a loss for is what to give Eric for birthdays and Christmas. Our bedroom is even painted Cardinal red.

When we moved to Houston, we bought a house in a neighborhood with excellent public schools. Eric and I believe there is a hand guiding us in life, and it turned out that the mascot for our children's new high school was none other than a cardinal.

Despite his lifelong obsession, Eric had never seen an actual live cardinal bird until we moved to Houston. Growing up in the U.S. Virgin Islands, he'd caught glimpses of them on TV, and he pictured them as red, fierce . . . and large.

One day while unpacking in our new house, I saw a male cardinal through the window. Nonchalantly, I called out to my sweetie, "Hey, Eric, there's a cardinal in our bird feeder."

Eric, whose physique looks like you would expect it to after twenty years of triathlon and cycling, pounded into the living room like a rhino instead of his usual cheetah self, wearing an expectant grin and not much else.

"WHERE IS IT?" he asked.

Lost for words, I pointed out our front window and prayed the elderly woman next door was not walking past our house.

"It's awfully small."

(That was Eric that said that, not the elderly neighbor.)

He was crestfallen. The mighty cardinal was a tiny slip of a bird.

But he stayed faithful, and to this day, the Cardinals are a big presence in our lives. As I look out the window into our front yard, I see the most beautiful (obnoxious) cardinal pinwheel in the flower bed, erected originally just to embarrass the kids. It worked great! It embarrassed me, too, and I'm sure it made the neighbors wildly jealous.

Ours is not to question why, ours is but to do or die.

Yes, cardinals.

THE NINJANATOR

Our we-moved-the-kids-away-from-paradise-guilt gift that first year in the states was a black mini lop-eared bunny. Because we didn't have enough pets already, right?

The kids named him Ninja. Ninja used the litter box and walked on a leash. Well, that's not totally true. He fought like a demon on a leash, but he did use the litter box when and how he felt like it, meaning he used it to launch litter all over the game room.

Ninja bonded with me while the kids were at school. He preferred females and was not crazy about Eric. What he preferred about females was their chests, as in "a conveniently soft place in which to sink one's razor-sharp bunny teeth."

Between protecting Ninja from the dogs and cat and dabbing Neosporin on our bite marks, I started to question the rabbit-purchase decision. What was that old saying? Marry in haste and repent at leisure? Yeah. I think it applies to buying rabbits, too.

HOMICIDE: 22 UNNAMED VICTIMS

AP Breaking News:

Wecare sad to report that twenty-two fish lost their lives to chlorine poisoning in a Houston backyard pond when a male resident of the household left water running into the pond. The bodies were discovered at about 2:00 p.m. by a traumatized resident, who first noticed something fishy when she saw a river rushing behind her bedroom's glass doors and up onto the deck. She will remain anonymous out of concern for her personal safety.

Upon investigation, the witness discovered a lake had formed in the backyard behind the music room. When she sought the source of the flooding, she came upon the grisly sight of twenty-two koi and goldfish belly-up in the lowest of the three ponds, with water spilling over the sides of said pond. She turned the water off and made efforts to revive the fish, but those efforts proved unsuccessful.

Among the casualties were a black "googly-eyed" fish and two fat calico fantail goldfish. Their bodies were removed with a cat litter scoop and respectfully disposed of in a plastic Kroger bag. A brief memorial service was conducted before the fish were solemnly laid to their final rest via deposit into the dumpster.

All household residents expressed shock, horror, and grief.

"Those fish grew up in our pond. They trusted us. They were part of our family. Did you know he killed one of our cats one time, too?" said Liz Hutchins.

"Huh, what fish?" asked Clark Jackson.

"Can we go to Petco on Saturday and get some more fish? How many can we get? How much can I spend? Can I bring a friend?" queried Susanne Jackson.

"I heard he emptied a black garbage bag of frogs into the bayou. I have to question what that was all about now," exclaimed Pamela Hutchins. "And there goes this month's water bill!"

Representatives for resident Eric Hutchins advised that he will be invoking his Fifth Amendment right to make no comment. They also wish to remind everyone that Eric was the hero that saved Cowboy.

Authorities stated that this is an ongoing investigation, but would not comment on whether the case of the dead cat has been reopened.

No charges have been filed at this time. Residents are advised to attend closely to their pets in the future, and to exercise caution when leaving them in the care of the adult male of the household.

FAMILY KILLING SPREE CONTINUES

Check out the email that Eric the animal killer sent to our sensitive children about our beautiful family cat, Juliet. Here's her picture in (slightly) better days:

Foreshadowing, though? Those are Eric's hands around her throat.

Here's Eric's email:

——Original Message——
From: Eric
To: Susanne
Cc: Clark; Pamela; Liz
Subject: Ju Ju
Check out this picture of Juu Juu

____

We all joke around about what a pain Juliet is, but we never really mean it. We all, especially Susanne, love our pets, and Eric sent this picture directly to her. This is a tragedy. I shook my head, hoping that someday they could all forgive Eric, and that Susanne would forgive me for marrying him. Or at least that they don't sock us with the bill for therapy. Or turn out just like him. I was hoping nobody would call Child Protective Services or the Society for Prevention of Cruelty to Animals, when—

Wait a second. Something was scratching at my office door.

Oops. False alarm! Here's JuJu, unharmed.

Still, a sick joke to pull on the kids.

But then again, that crazy sense of humor is one of the things I love about him most. And, with therapy, the children will recover.

JEALOUSY

When Juliet went missing one day, Susanne was distraught. The rest of us? Well, we felt bad for Susanne. Juliet drives us a little bonkers.

Juliet is very jealous of Ninja, and that may be why she bolted. That or because Eric locked her in the downstairs bathroom overnight when Grandma visited. Maybe both.

Juliet is a beautiful cat, but a bit needy and emotionally erratic. We hope she found a lovely home with no rabbits or grandparents. Maybe Eric's email to the kids was foreshadowing after all?

THE NINJCOMPOOP

Above: Ninja watching TV from underneath the coffee table

Ninja, AKA Buns of Steel, AKA Bunnicula the bloodsucking bunny, soon began to hang out under our coffee table and make dashes out around the living room and up and over furniture and people. He seemed to especially enjoy watching football and was really sad when the Jags and Cowboys lost. He was bummed there were no professional football teams named after his kind—the Hares, the Bunnies, the Rabbits, even the Bucks. He showed some partiality toward Tampa Bay Buccaneers—possibly because of the name?

AT LEAST THE DOG FEELS GREAT.

The preparations for Eric's business trips to India are intense. He has to get his visa, work out "in-country" {Domestic transportation from one place to another while in the foreign country, India in this instance. } travel plans to several cities, make decisions about security, and go to the doctor for shots and prescription medications. One of the prescriptions he always gets is Cipro, a powerful antibiotic.

A few days before Eric left one time, Karma came down with what looked like a foot infection. Since our vet bills tend to be scandalous, Eric decided he would take matters into his own hands. He diligently researched the issue on the internet and learned that an appropriate dose of Cipro could treat the condition. (Kids, don't try this at home.)

So he gave Karma the Cipro . . . or at least, what he thought was the Cipro. Actually, he accidentally gave her the anti-diarrheal medicine first. Her feet weren't any better, but she did have really solid poop. Then he figured out the error and switched her to the real Cipro.

Off Eric went to India. His flight from Newark to Mumbai was sixteen hours long. About halfway through his flight, two of our three at-home kids came down with the flu. Eric happened to come down with it at the same time, somewhere over the Atlantic. He got to

Mumbai at about ten p.m. and waited through long lines in immigra-
tion in a posture of near-death with no medications available, but
then his kindly driver took him to get the Indian facsimile of Pepto-
Bismol—called, I kid you not, VOMISTOP—and Theraflu. He finally
arrived at his hotel nearly twenty-four hours after he started, and sick
as a dog, so to speak.

Two long days of high-stakes meetings, travel by planes, trains,
and automobile across India, and three sleepless nights later in
Jamnagar, he finally got to visit a doctor. He was staying in a refinery
compound of seven hundred houses and one large guest "house," a
giant spa-like structure with marble, fountains, a restaurant, a
workout facility, and the coup d'état, a twenty-four-hour clinic with a
real doctor. The doctor was free, the prescription cost only $1.99. The
medication: Cipro.

I am pleased to report that both Eric and the dog recovered just
fine.

THE PRODIGAL CAT

When Juliet returned home after two weeks on the lam, Susanne was tearfully happy; the other four of us groaned. After her sabbatical in the wilderness of the Meyerland {An area mostly populated by old Jewish people. Not exactly Wild Kingdom.} subdivision of Houston, Juliet was even more emotionally unbalanced than usual. She meowed constantly and refused to be alone in a room by herself—*God forbid* in the house by herself. If we tried to leave, she yowled and launched herself at us, hanging onto our clothes by every claw on all four feet. The first time she tried this with Eric, he met her midsection with the sole of his foot, so she pestered the rest of us more {It could be that Eric's popular demonstration of "spin the kitty" on her back on the tile floor also has something to do with her willingness to give him a wide berth.} to make up for it. At least she was willing to pay for this togetherness with affection; our newfound snuggle-kitty used to not let anyone hold her.

Ninja ignored her, and vice versa. It looked like we were back to being a five-mammalian-pet family. I'd count the non-mammals, too, but oops—all the fish are dead.

URBAN JUNGLE

So maybe Meyerland wasn't Wild Kingdom, but it wasn't the animal-less concrete morass I had feared when we moved here. Not only because of our abundance of domestic animal life, either. There was wildlife as well. Our multi-ponded rainforest-esque backyard attracted wilderness refugees galore.

We had the frogs, of course, Lord help us we had the frogs. But it wasn't just them. Our first summer we kept seeing turtles in the grass bayous that ran along South Rice, about where it turned into Rutherglenn {I will not digress here into a diatribe against the naming conventions of Houston streets, other than to say it is the norm for streets to suddenly change names for no apparent reason.}. We assisted one in relocating into our back yard. That didn't last, because the turtle didn't appreciate the loving attentions of Karma, Layla, and Cowboy. We also saw big nutria {Large swamp rodents that look like giant rats, but with rounder bodies. Say it with me: ewwwwww.} in the bayous, but I vetoed any attempts to relocate them.

From our breakfast table, we watched the antics of squirrels desperate to breach the ramparts of the bird feeder in our Gone With The Wind-like front yard trees. Occasionally we ate breakfast in our great room instead so we could see the backyard version, this time played out over our ponds. We went through a series of supposedly squirrel-proof bird feeders. If you've ever gone through this exercise, you know there ain't no such thing. However, we found one that almost worked. It had a domed hood of clear plastic over a smallish feeder that dangled about 18 inches below the dome. The squirrels would stage assaults for hours, getting braver, smarter, and more pissed off as time wore on. Ultimately, several squirrels managed daring leaps from side branches and acrobatic maneuvers down the dome and under it to clutch the feeder in triumph. Their joy was short-lived, however. When they would finish eating, to a man the squirrels would jump straight up toward the nearest limb. Oops. Plastic dome. Squirrel in pond. Squirrel frantically swimming. Squirrel rapidly exiting, looking like an embarrassed long skinny drowned rat. Never did we see a repeat attempt by a squirrel after the dome-to-water dunking.

Besides the squirrels (and an occasional rat), the animals we saw most frequently were birds, an astounding variety of birds. We saw cranes, egrets, and other bayou fowl. I loved the ringed kingfisher, in his dress whites and bow tie. Cardinals, robins, blue jays, and red-headed woodpeckers entertained us. Red-tailed hawks chased smaller, frantic birds through our yard and their prey would crash into our windows. *Time to look away, kids.* Once a hawk stunned a dove, which fell into our pond. It was still alive, so we carried it into our game room and wrapped it in a towel, leaving it on the ping pong table. Yes, we shut the doors to keep the dogs and cat out. When the dove revived, it revived with a vengeance and it took a full family effort to herd it back outside through the wide-open double French doors. Eric cleaned up the mess it left behind.

At night, the power lines behind our house were a mammalian superhighway. We could only see their silhouettes, but identified them by their shapes as possums, rats, and raccoons. Sometimes we'd hear them on the balcony outside Liz's room, scritching and scratching. A time or two we heard them up in the attic and inside the walls. Thank God they found their own way out 'without help from Lone Star Rodent Removal. (At least I didn't smell the evidence if they did not.)

For a home office goddess like myself, the view is one of the perks. And as a girl raised on *Ranger Rick*, I couldn't have asked more of Meyerland.

GOOD KARMA OR BAD KARMA?

When we were living at Annaly, isolated in the rainforest on St. Croix, six large dogs and two cats (and one short-lived pig) made perfect sense for security and pest control. However, when we moved to the house in Houston with a normal-sized backyard, we had to downsize our pet population. You will recall that we took three dogs and one cat {It will surprise no one who is familiar with Eric's track record with cats that Eric "gave Tiger away to a really good home"—which is grownup talk for "foisted her on a six-year-old kid playing in his family's front yard, then drove away like a bat out of hell." Just kidding.} to Texas. The total dog weight was still close to three hundred pounds, though. Count up the pounds with me: Cowboy, a mutant yellow lab the size of a pony, weighed 125 pounds; Layla, a sweet boxer and Cowboy's "girl," weighed 65; and Karma, a clingy German shepherd obsessed with Eric, weighed 85. {Eric's daughter Marie called her Karmela, as she seemed to want to be Eric's wife, too.} Yowza.

That first summer, the dog poop got insane. I cannot adequately convey the horror of standing amidst fly-covered piles of poop on our deck while cooking steaks at the grill. Imagine a Cambodian minefield, and you might get close. Even with the kids picking up two to three times a week, it is bad when you have nearly three hundred pounds of pup. We knew that three big dogs were too many and one had to go. That one, we decided, was Karma, since Layla is Marie's dog, and Cowboy is Layla's boyfriend and Susanne's bestie.

For her swan song, Karma came down with a serious case of hereditary mange. It normally occurs in a dog's first year of life, if at all, but whaddya gonna do, she got it at two. It had to be cured before she could be outsourced. The mange started with swollen bloody feet and turned into hairless, weepy patches all over her body. We kept Karma in the house for nearly two weeks—which is worse than it sounds, as she was never housebroken. She'd lived up at Annaly as an outside guard dog, after all.

We initialized a regimen: wash her feet in hydrogen peroxide, goop her up with Neosporin, and dope her up with Benadryl. But it didn't cure her, and the stench from her wounds and her bathroom habits finally forced us to kick her back outside and take her to the vet, which, I kid you not, cost close to a thousand dollars by the time we were through. All of this just to get rid of her. The vet kept ordering tests without our permission that we didn't want [to pay for], and on the day of her third treatment, Karma vomited, so they gave her a seventy-dollar shot in case it was an allergic reaction—even though she hadn't been allergic to the treatment the first two times. We felt robbed.

Layla had also had serious hereditary mange, you may recall. Sadly, it appears the two breeds most susceptible to autoimmune disorders are, according to our very well-paid vet, boxers and German shepherds. The vet asked if we by any chance had a rottweiler, too, as those are the third most susceptible. Bullet dodged: we had one— Callia—until we left St. Croix.

As we were dealing with Karma's mange in Texas, a year after we'd left St. Croix, Annaly was finally under contract. That left us looking for homes for two dogs, not just Karma: Jake {I would love to say Jake did a fine job as a guard dog for us that last year, except that we got robbed to the tune of $50,000 on his watch, so I think I'll just say instead that he enjoyed his time there and didn't tear the place up too much. Hrmph.} was the last dog standing at Annaly and was in need of a forever home. He got lucky and was adopted (hopefully permanently) by our house sitters.

Encouraged by our success, we advertised Karma online in Houston. This nice young couple with a puppy came and got her that day at about 5:30. They really loved her; it was so great. By 9:30 they'd left a message asking to bring her back, and when we woke up the next morning she was in our driveway in her kennel, looking tired and embarrassed. Poor Karma. Apparently, she *whined* at night. Shocking that a dog would do that on the first night in a new place. So, we tried again.

One day later, a very large older woman came to visit Karma, and it was love at first sight for both of them. Karma was singing opera for her within five minutes, which is one of her happy tricks. The woman wanted Karma for companionship and protection. I repeated "she is not house trained" over and over, and the woman swore that was OK, she would take care of her. She said she had a big walk-in shower to bathe her in, which is great because Karma loves water. I crossed my fingers and loaded Karma in the truck, but I knew it would be OK. (Yep, I could feel the good karma.)

Don't tell anyone, but I cried a little when she was gone.

HOME OFFICE MATES

D^{ogs, dem.}

Juliet shared an office with the dogs and me in Houston. Of course, she did not permit herself to be photographed in the same frame as them. She wanted me to point out that Ninja does not have the honor of sharing office space with the rest of us. Juliet may be a cat, but she can be a real bitch.

RIP, MY FINE-FEATHERED FRIEND.

I am a planner. I plan and schedule and plot, much to the delight of my engineer/cyclist husband, who loves to live by a plan. Even more, he loves for me to make a plan and then for us both to live by it. And what he loves most of all is when the plan I make and live by includes a healthy dose of us bicycling and swimming together. I believe a plan is a structure within which to make reasonable changes, while Eric casts his plans in cement. Obviously I am right, so there usually isn't much of a problem.

But I did not plan what happened to us in the Good Old Summertime Classic, a sixty-nine-mile bicycle ride along some of our most favorite roads for cycling, anywhere. The bike route runs in and around Fayetteville, Texas, including the tiny old town of Roundtop. We had trained for it. We had talked about it with joy and reverence. Eric even accidentally went to get our packets a full week before they were available for pick-up (don't ask).

The night before the race, I developed a PMS {Technically, I suffer from PMDD – Pre-Menstrual Dysphoric Disorder – but try to say, "I'm feeling PMDDy" or "I'm really PMDDing right now." Yeah. It doesn't exactly roll off the tongue.} aka hormonal migraine. Because it was the middle of the night, I took one of my gentler migraine prescriptions, hoping that this pill plus sleep would be all I needed. I woke up at 5:00 a.m. to the mother of all migraines. I caved in and went for the elephant tranquilizer. Unfortunately, I was so nauseous from the migraine, I couldn't eat. My husband, a man of immense patience and even greater kindness, suggested we stay home.

But we had made a plan, so I got in the car anyway under the theory that I had no idea now how I would feel in two and a half hours. Although I kinda did know, and just didn't want to admit it.

I should have listened to my husband.

On the way to the race, driving in the dark, the unthinkable happened. I had my head on Eric's shoulder, sweetly sleeping (make that "snoring and drooling under the influence of the elephant pill"), when he let out a tiny swear word. Actually, I believe it started with an F, and was preceded by the word "mother," and that his voice blasted through my cranium and echoed madly inside my impaired brain.

"What happened?" I screamed, heart pounding, hand clutching throat, eyes sweeping the road for signs of the apocalypse.

"I hit a cardinal."

OH MY GOD. HE HIT A CARDINAL.

Since the time he could speak, my husband has proclaimed himself a fan of the ~~ChicagoPhoenix St. Louis~~ Arizona Cardinals football team. His screen saver at work has always been a giant Cardinal ~~head~~ logo, until very recently when he finally switched it to a picture of us, under teensy-tinsy little applications of subtle pressure from me. He watched their playoff game in 2009 at 2:00 a.m. through a webcam picture of our TV on his laptop in his hotel room in Libya. He collects cardinals and Cardinal paraphernalia and insists on displaying them prominently in our bedroom.

Back to ear-splitting expletives and wife-under-the-influence. "Honey, I didn't feel an impact. Are you sure you didn't miss it?" I asked.

"They're awfully small birds," he said.

Ahhhh, good point. We drove on somberly. We arrived at the race. I stumbled off to the bathroom. When I came back, Eric was crouched in front of the grill of our car. I joined him, confused. He held up a handful of tiny red feathers.

I swear it was the drugs, but I burst out laughing. "You, you of all people, you killed a *cardinal*?"

He glared at me as he picked the biggest and brightest of the small feathers and tucked it reverently into the chest strap of his heart monitor. "I'm going to carry this feather with me in tribute, the whole way."

So we got on our bikes: me, wobbly, cotton-mouthed, and somewhat delirious; Eric, solemn and determined. This, the ride for the cardinal, would be the ride of his life. Sixty-nine miles to the glory of the cardinal.

I made it all of about two miles before I apologized. "I'm anaerobic, and we're only going twelve miles per hour on a flat. I'm really messed up from these drugs."

"You can do it, honey. We came all this way. Now we're riding for a higher purpose."

I gave it my best, I really did, but a few miles later, after a succession of hills where going up with a racing heartbeat was only slightly less awful than cruising down with a seriously messed-up sense of balance, I pulled to a stop.

"I've never quit before, but I can't do it today, love."

A beautiful male cardinal swooped across the road in front of us. Eric bit his lip. "I understand. Do you want to flag a SAG [support and aid] wagon?"

"I can make it back if we just take it easy. I'm sorry, honey."

My husband treated me like a princess that day, but all the excitement had drained out of him. This race we had planned for was not to be. And a teacup-sized bird had sacrificed his life in vain, because I had overdosed on Immitrex and ruined the plan. The waste of it all, the waste of a day, the waste of a life: it was hard to overcome. But Eric tried; I'll give him credit for that, the man really tried.

That night, after we did a make-up ride on the trainer while we watched *We Are Marshall* (interrupted occasionally by Eric's sobs, because the only thing worse than a dead cardinal is a dead football player), I pulled our sheets out of the drier and brought them into our room. Eric—wearing his new Fayetteville Good Old Summertime T-shirt—helped me put the warm, clean cotton on the bed.

As we hoisted the sheets in the air to spread them out over the mattress, a tiny red feather shot straight up toward the light and wafted down slowly, back and forth, back and forth, until, pushed by the soft breeze of our ceiling fan, it landed on the pillow on Eric's side of the bed.

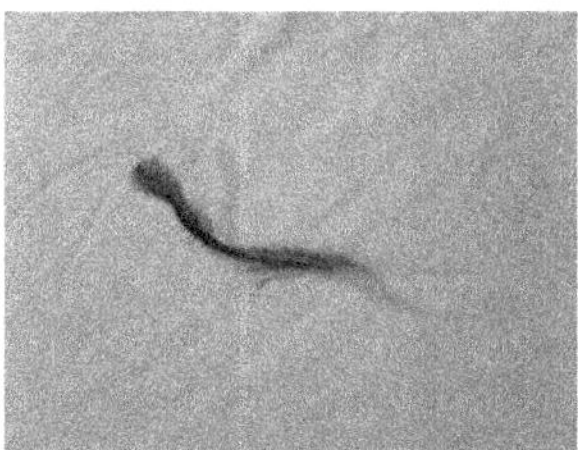

Above: Actual cardinal feather on Eric's pillow.

Steeling myself for the worst, I shot a glance at him to see if he had noticed. I did not exhale. Maybe I had time to brush it off quickly? Too late—he was staring at the feather. "Is that damn bird going to haunt me for the rest of my life now?" But he smiled.

"Probably. You did senselessly murder a cardinal, Eric."

And he laughed. And we began to talk about our plans for the Tour de Pepper ride the next weekend, a ride where, I hoped, we would not cause the death of any of God's creatures. Or at least nothing but an armadillo.

CRACKHEAD POSSUM
MOVES IN

One day, shortly before noon in broad daylight, Eric and I came upon a strange sight. Weaving down the middle of our street toward us, its eyes glazed and fixed, its feet stumbling, came a possum. Not just any possum, but a big, scraggly possum. A possum that looked like an overgrown rat sick with radiation poisoning and male-pattern baldness. I kind of think they all look that way, but anyway, it was an ugly possum.

This possum was confused. Possums, or "opossums" as those with more class than me call them, are nocturnal creatures. Either this one suffered from jet lag (having just arrived on a direct flight from Mumbai, possibly?), or it had mistaken day for night.

"Poor possum. He needs to go home and go to bed. Do you think there's something wrong with him?" I asked. I popped a handful of macadamia nuts into my mouth and concentrated on their salty yumminess.

"Maybe she doesn't have a home," Eric said.

"Maybe he did have a home, but his possum wife kicked him out because he never shut any cabinets," I said, nodding my head.

"Maybe her possum husband booted her azz because she writes a blog about his fictitious gender-confusion issues and Ironman underpants," Eric suggested, his eyebrows arched into points.

"Or maybe he's on crack, and he's jacking the neighborhood cars for loose change," I said. We live in a nice neighborhood, but our cars have been broken into twice recently, so it's not as far-fetched as it sounds.

So we carefully dodged said possum and pulled into our driveway. But we couldn't get it out of our minds. Later that day, Eric, ever the softie, took a bowl of dog food out into our front yard. The possum stumbled drunkenly to the bowl and had a meal. When it was done, Eric moved the bowl to the back yard. Theoretically, our two hundred pounds of doggies live there, but they are far too spoiled to eat outside. The possum dined in peace.

That night, we heard noises out back. "What's that?" I whispered. My stomach twisted with nerves. I moved closer to Eric, my nose practically under his armpit, which gave me a comforting whiff of Irish Spring body wash.

Scritch-scritch-scritch-scritch. Something was scratching the back wall of our bedroom. Something possibly out of a Stephen King movie, or worse. Something that would drag us from our beds and eat our brains, leaving behind only the empty skulls and the words "Juicy Couture" scrawled in our blood across our deck. I dived in for another huff of Irish Spring.

"I think our crackhead friend is trying to move in," Eric said.

It took me a moment, but I realized he meant the possum. "IN, in? Can he get in?"

"No, she won't make it. I'll let the dogs out to chase her off."

"NO! You fed him, we can't let the dogs out there. They'll kill him." I should have seen this coming.

We debated, but in the end we decided to leave it alone. *Our casa es su casa*, I whispered. *Feliz navidad, poco opossum.* Call it restitution for the frogs.

PILLOW FIGHT

A photo of sweet JuJu, who usurped the dog pillows and enjoyed the fire. The giant canines were too scared of the slightly unbalanced cat to challenge her.

JuJu got up to use her box, though, and Cowboy and Layla tiptoed in and stole their spots back. Such big, brave doggies.

After the dogs reclaimed the pillows, anyone want to guess what the cat did next? Hint: Rhymes with "slay" but has a "pr" in it. Yeah. I did an extra load of laundry. The battle was on. Just another exciting day at the home office.

OUR DOG WHISPERER

Cowboy the Big Yellow Dog has a lethal tail and a bony head like a dinosaur. Eric sometimes calls him Chewbacca—not because of his size, but because he talks like Chewbacca. A lot.

Cowboy's heart has always belonged to Susanne. At 120+ pounds apiece with silky blond hair, they are a great match. Susanne loves to curl up with him nose to nose. He wraps his paws around her arms to make sure she doesn't leave him.

When Susanne would ask him, "Do you love me?," he would answer in Chewbacca noises that sounded shockingly like "I love you."

"Do you love only me?" she asked.

Chewbacca responded with something that sounded quite similar to "yes."

"Do you love me so much, more than anything in the world?" she asked, and again he replied. This would go on for five or six iterations of question and answer until they tired of the game.

I tried to recreate the scene myself once. I slipped into Susanne's position next to Cowboy and asked, "Do you love me?" His eyes smiled, and he wacked his tail like a club against the ground, but he did not answer. "Do you love Eric?" Nothing. "Are you a good dog?"

Silence. "Do you love Susanne?" Chewbacca agreed enthusiastically with a loud "Rarrr rarrr rarrrr."

The only thing he ever says to me—and he says it each day at eleven a.m.—is "out."

Forget Cesar Millan. That girl is the Dog Whisperer.

RAPTORS 1, INDUSTRY 0

Eric was supposed to do some work at an oil refinery in St. Paul, but it was indefinitely postponed. It seemed that one of only three pairs of mating peregrine falcons in the state of Minnesota had made their home in the exact stripper {No, that's not another name for an exotic cage dancer. A stripper tower is a piece of equipment in a refinery.} tower of the exact fluid catalytic cracking unit that his team was scheduled to work on. The refinery was working with state agencies on a relocation for the birds, but it appeared Eric's trip would have to at least wait for the little hatchlings to arrive.

How would you like to be the guy that took this picture? That bird looks like it is ready to do some damage. The operators from this refinery reported that any time they got near this tower, she and her mate dive-bombed them. Also, see the band on her leg? She had been tagged and was being tracked.

Note that she placed the eggs the perfect distance from the warm toasty flange in the upper left. She didn't even have to sit on these eggs, and no need for a nest. Girl Power!

NEW FAVORITE PET

After sweeping animal hair from tile floors every other day for eight years, I decided something had to give. I tried making the kids take over, but they missed spots or sometimes just skipped the entire exercise. I wanted something as tireless as Cowboy, as eager to please as Layla, and as independent as Juliet. So I found a favorite new pet. No, it was not the rabbit, although I sort of loved him. It was the Roomba robotic floor cleaner! It followed me around the house, talked to me, didn't make a mess—and in fact, cleaned up after others, did what it was told when it was told, and went to its bed for a time-out when it was tired.

I found myself talking to it: "Way to go, little buddy!" or "Great job in the living room!" Sometimes "Do you need a rest?" and "How about I clean those filters for you?" Embarrassing but true. I could go on and on about this clever little thing, but I'll spare you.

Pet shmet. It was my new favorite child.

NOT A BEAVER

Every day when she came home from school, the first thing Susanne did was pick up the rabbit and snuggle it, pet it, carry it around, shove it in my face, and try to put it on my bed, because "he just wants to come see you, Mommy." And every day after Beelzebunny bit her, Susanne would go into my bathroom for the hydrogen peroxide, cotton balls, band-aids, and Neosporin. She was as unconcerned about the daily biting as she was about leaving the first aid supplies all over my counter. On this particular day, though, she had something different to tell me.

"Mom, I can't find Ninja."

This didn't sound like especially bad news to me. Just that morning when Eric went into Bunnicula's domain to feed him, he'd found him asleep in the cat box, which the cat had been using for several days for cat box purposes. Ninjapoo had gotten all tuckered out after digging to China; litter and unmentionables were scattered all around the room.

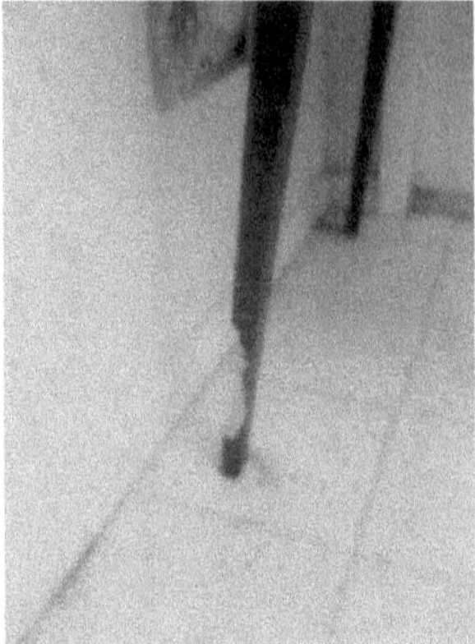

Only one day before, said hare had displayed another charming quality: the gnawing ability of a beaver five times his size. In that one day alone, Eric repaired four bunny-bitten cords: my elliptical trainer and three cords to our Wii and its various accessories. And Thumper had already eaten through extension cords and lamp cords, and even destroyed a plugged-in laptop entirely.

The bunny's charms were wearing thin.

So, I answered my daughter with the memories of Ninja's bad behavior in my mind. "I'm sure he's just hiding from you. We'll find him when Eric gets home. In the meantime, I need you to finish your homework and pack a bag. The Weather Channel said we're going to have a hurricane."

"Cool," she said. A hurricane was nothing new or scary to my island girl. If anything, it was, well, cool.

That afternoon, I wrote a post to my blog, bemoaning the bunny's flaws and making fun of him for his beaver impersonation. I lamented that if we left town to avoid the hurricane, he'd have to ride the storm out alone. When Eric came home, I told him about Ninja's AWOL status.

Eric is a methodical searcher. Susanne is our finder of all things, but with her that's all intuition-based. Eric hunts for the missing like he's a crime scene specialist on *CSI* with a search grid and an ultraviolet light. He made a first pass of the house. No Ninja.

"Could he have gotten outside when a door was open?" I asked.

"Maybe. I searched the front and back yards, though, too. No sign of him," Eric replied.

After dinner, Eric resumed the hunt. Now he took it to another level. Furniture was moved. Doors presumed closed were opened anyway and he combed their interior rooms. Attic spaces were searched. Meanwhile, after I shepherded the kids into packing their "just in case" Hurricane Ike travel bags, I did what I normally do in the evenings when we aren't training or supervising kids: I stole a few moments to write. Forty-five minutes later, when I was lost in the world of Annalise and Katie, Eric came into my office and shut the door behind him.

"I found him," he said. His tone and face said that his good news wasn't.

"Oh no," I replied.

"He was behind the weight bench. Stiff, or starting to be anyway. Like the guinea pig[footnote]Note again the common link in pet deaths, too numerous to recount in full in this book. Makes me wonder: where was Eric when Chester the pig died, hmm?[/footnote] was when I found it dead in its cage back on St. Croix."

"What in the world? He was fine this morning."

"I don't know," he said, "but I have a theory."

"The cat poop?" I asked, then immediately felt silly. That made no sense. "Did he throw his back out doing a crazy bunny gainer twisty hop?" That didn't seem right either. Rabbits were born to do that maneuver.

"I think that table leg he chewed yesterday did him in."

"But how?"

"Maybe a varnish on the wood? Maybe he couldn't pass wood through his digestive system. My money's on the varnish, though. It's poisonous."

Unbelievable. An overdose of wood chips did him in? This was horrible. Worse, I felt guilty, oh so guilty. I had groused about the bunny. Worse yet, I had regretted that we got him. I hadn't exactly wanted him to die a horrible and premature death from poisoned wood chips, but still.

"And another thing," Eric said. "I caught the news a minute ago. We need to leave for Austin if we're going. We can stay for the storm if you want to, but they're not calling for a mandatory evacuation. It just seems like if there were ever a good excuse to go visit Marie, this would be it."

"Yes, of course, let's go."

We assembled the children hastily and told them we were leaving to visit their sister at the University of Texas, STAT—and, oh yeah, the rabbit died. Other than morbid curiosity about the circumstances, the kids took the news well. They'd received news of a lot of dead pets in their time. By now, hurricane evacuation had their undivided attention, so poor Ninja was given a very rapid service and burial in a shallow, unmarked grave.

I do want to assure everyone that we'd always given him bunny-recommended and bunny-appropriate chew toys, and we encouraged him to play with those instead of eat the furniture. Unfortunately, the force of his personality was stronger than we were.

Ah, the guilt.

RIP, Bunnicula.

REDNECK ADVENTURES

S o my long-suffering island-boy-to-Texas-transplant husband convinced me that the perfect retreat for our family would be in a secondhand {Make that thirdhand, but who's counting} trailer on a bug- and snake-infested piece of property five miles from Nowheresville, Texas—yeah, for real—much to the chagrin of our kids, especially Clark, who announced that his weekends were 100% booked from now until infinity in Houston with debate, robotics, and a girlfriend.

We looked for Texas Hill Country acreage for quite some time. The conversation between my husband and me about this one went something like this:

Eric: I lahhhhke this one. It has a POND on it.

Me: Stop me if I've said this before: Some cowboy is going to kick your ass and good one of these days for making fun of our accents. And ponds have snakes.

Eric: That pond is nahhhhhhce. I lahhhhhhke that pond.

Me: I like that it is only an hour and a half from your office.

Eric: And it has a real nahhhhhce pond.

Me: I think you've mentioned that. But I can't camp out there. Too many bugs and snakes. And Africa-hot. Plus there's those bugs and snakes.

Eric: We'll get us a travel-trailer. That'd be nahhhhhhce. You'd lahhhhhhke it.

Me: Forget the cowboy. *I'm* going to kick your ass. And I made a promise to myself years ago—no RVs, no travel trailers. Sheets, running water, A/C, indoor potties, and no trailers.

Eric: You're not being very nahhhhhce.

(Sounds of scuffle and pummeling, and Clark laughing at seeing his mother beating the crud out of his stepdad.)

Well, of course we bought the land, which we dubbed Shangri-La. Then we bought and fetched the trailer of a redneck's dreams from a real nahhhhhce couple even further away from Nowheresville, Texas. It came time for Bubba-mon, Clark, and me {Clark's sisters conveniently found ways out of helping. Not that their help was ever much help, anyway.} to stash the trailer—soon dubbed the Quacker because *Mallard* was emblazoned on its front window cover—on Shangri-La.

Surprise, surprise, we had some issues.

First, five minutes before we got there, we took a shortcut detour which, it turned out, included an overhead bridge under which our trailer could not pass. As we turned around to take the long way, Cowboy whimpered once, shot Bubba-mon an apologetic look in the rear view mirror, and unloaded the entire contents of his freakishly large digestive system out his back end and down the spare tire well of our 2000 Suburban. This is how we discovered, to Clark's eternal horror, that four hours really is Cowboy's limit in the car. Oops, had it been that long?

Second, a mere thirty minutes later, this is how Clark discovered that no matter how logical it seems to him, toilet bowl cleaner is not the appropriate thing to use to clean dog poo from your vehicle's carpet. No, we don't always carry toilet bowl cleaner with us. We had stocked up on supplies for the Quacker. Luckily, those supplies included alternative cleaners to deal with the vaporized carpet.

Third, as my Bubba-mon pulled downhill on our narrow, winding drive into Shangri-La, he swung wide to avoid planting the Quacker into a tree. This is how we discovered the large tree stump *under* the skinny bush that he had assumed the Suburban would easily skim over.

Fourth, when Bubba-mon was unable to free the Suburban from its high-center position on the stump through techniques such as teeter-tottering forward and backward, lifting, and lightening the load, Clark, after many unhelpful and highly irritating suggestions, came up with one good one. He suggested we use our jack to achieve clearance and then gently pull off and over the jack. This is how we discovered that there was no jack in the Suburban, after all. I'm not going to blame the teenage driver of this Suburban, but, well, there is the issue of custodial possession and responsibility. *If you're reading this, Liz, honey, I love you, and all is forgiven.*

Long story short, Bubba-mon ultimately decided that the stump and Suburban were conjoined at a noncritical area, and he got aggressive with the gas pedal. It worked. He employed his superior trailer-backing skills, and we hid the Quacker in the woods and headed home to Houston. Where we slept like the freakin' dead.

Three weekends later, we loaded up the truck and we moved to Beverly . . . Shangri-La that is, big ponds, bugs and snakes (cue banjo music). Of course, we ran into a few issues.

Upon entering the trailer, a horrible smell assaulted my princess-and-the-pea-like nose. Since the trailer had sat in the sun for weeks in the Texas heat, this was not entirely unexpected. Yet, somehow it was. Unexpected. And really, really awful.

Me: There's something dead in here, Eric.

Bubba-mon: Turn on the A/C. You've got an overly-sensitive nose. It's probably just musty.

Five minutes pass. Meanwhile, Clark made a tactical error: he flushed our brand-new thirdhand potty. A noxious odor filled the trailer. The LP gas detector went off immediately, screeching out its warning to everyone within a five-mile radius.

Me: (running from trailer with towel over my face, Clark on my heels, gagging) OH GOD OH GOD OH GOD OH GOD RUN ERIC RUN IT'S GOING TO BLOW

Bubba-mon: (running) (IN THE WRONG DIRECTION) What the hell's going on?

Me: I don't know. Clark flushed the potty, it got really stinky, and the alarm went off. I'm afraid we have a propane leak. We have to evacuate.

Bubba-mon: Hmmmmm, but the propane isn't even turned on. (Sticks head foolishly into trailer.) Oh SHIT. What's that smell? (Turns to me.) OH, shit. That's methane gas. (Reaches over and turns off LP gas detector.)

Me: What do we do?

Bubba-mon: I can fix this, no problem. {This was the first time we were to hear what became an oft-repeated phrase in the adventures of Bubba-mon and the Quacker in Nowheresville.}

So, first, this is how we discovered that, despite the instructions on the toilet tank treatment bottles that promise one dosage takes care of a whole load, you can't leave *anything* in that tank in the hundred-degree Texas sun for three weeks. We could have driven a Prius to Houston and back on the amount of methane we discharged into that twenty-six-foot trailer. Ace Ventura's "Whew, do not go in there!" took on a whole new meaning for us that day.

Second, after a honeymoon phase that lasted until darkness fell and the strangely disturbing night calls of the [7,521,999] frogs began, Cowboy and Layla crawled under the Quacker and cried half the night, until they finally moved closer to the thundering white noise of the generator, beside which they dug sleeping pits and curled up against its motherly presence like two puppies. And this is how we discovered that city dogs—like city girls—grow soft and become great big pansies after a few years away from the Cruzan rainforest.

Despite all of this, or maybe because of it—I dunno—I will grudgingly admit that Bubba-mon was right: This place is nahhh-hhce and I lahhhhhke it. I am head over heels for the Quacker,

Shangri-La, and Nowheresville.

HOW DO I LOVE THEE?

I am cheap. No, not *that* kind of cheap. I am fiscally tight. Notoriously so. Hold that thought; it's important to a story I want to tell you about Cowboy.

We went out to Nowheresville recently. Yeah, it was awesome, as usual. We even lured Eric's youngest daughter and her boyfriend into coming with us. We ran and biked; they fished and swam. We saw five black wild boars with a bevy of white piglets. We cooked out and made s'mores over a bonfire under the stars. Liz and I picked june bugs out of our food. The men carried the heavy things. It was all good.

Things went awry when Eric turned on the A/C in the Quacker. Or, rather, when he attempted to turn on the A/C, and realized it no longer C'd the A, so to speak. So off he trekked to Home Depot. He toted back a schnazzy portable A/C. Since it was ninety degrees (on March 26th!), I applauded this decision. I did not know we had a few more expenditures to go along the way.

Our next calamity struck when the generator came to a grinding halt. Oopsie. Out of gas? Nooo. Out of OIL. Bad. Dead generator. Cha-ching.

But the big tragedy of the weekend, while expensive, cost more in terms of fear and suffering than dollars. Cowboy, bless his little heart, got snakebit right between the toes on one of his front paws. We didn't know at the time that it was a snakebite, because we didn't see it happen. At first we thought he stepped on a thorn. But when his paw swelled up to look like a cow's hoof and all the poor animal could do was lay on his side in a fever and moan, you didn't have to be Steve Irwin to know something more had happened. By this time it was Sunday night, though, so we veterinarianized him ourselves, with some advice from my Dr. Dad. Mostly this consisted of rubbing his tummy, cooing to him, and soaking his paw in hot water. The paw went poof in the hot water and a cloud of yellowy gunk came out. I let Eric take care of that part, because it made him feel manly. And because I nearly vomited.

The next morning, the swelling had gone down considerably, but he still sported a fever and wanted us to know it. My gosh, that dog is talkative, even when he's sick. He couldn't put weight on it, and it looked awful. We were really worried about him. So I took him to the vet.

Now, long history makes me terrified of the financial implications of entering a veterinary office. This whole Cowboy-snake fiasco reminded me of vet visits gone by, with Layla and with Karma. The vet we took Karma to in Houston had a way of not only overcharging us, but also making us feel like the lowest form of dog-and-cat-owning humanity on earth when we didn't want to upgrade every service they offered to the limousine-and-caviar level. We are awesome pet owners. We love animals. However, we do not think they poop gold bricks. They're our pets, not our children. With apologies to people who believe their pets *are* their kids, we find it unavoidable to spend a much greater portion of our income on the human offspring than the canines and felines. That's just the way it has to be, because of that whole not pooping gold bricks thing. Sometimes we like the canines and felines better than the humans, but still we have no choice.

That night, I went on a desperate internet search for a new vet, but I didn't get very far Googling "veterinarians who don't think your pets poop gold bricks." Eric came to the rescue. He had noticed a small house with a veterinary clinic in it about fifteen minutes from our house, in a more rural and less high-income area. The online reviews of the vet were of the "walks on water" variety. I was at their door at 7:30 the next morning after lifting 125-pound Cowboy in and out of the back of our Suburban to get him there. Man, I'm glad I took up swimming and weight lifting.

The only comments they made when I walked in?

Nurse: "Oh my, that's a very big dog."

Vet: "Oh wow, your dog is large. I'm glad he's friendly."

"Why, yes. Yes, he is," I said.

This vet rocked. Seriously, y'all. If you need a vet in Houston, I'm the one to call for a referral. I felt like the by-God queen of all pet owners when I left, and I gave them only $165.37 for the visit, his antibiotic shot, and a bag of painkillers, ointment, and amoxicillin. Add to that the $4.39 cents I spent on chamomile-scented spa-foot-bath Epsom salts, and throw in a smidgen for a pair of cotton tube socks, baggies, and some masking tape, and that's it. No unnecessary platinum-plated treatment suggestions, and no "you must buy a doggie treadmill for this tub of goo along with a $2 million special prescription available-here-only diet dog food immediately or you will go to hell" lecture. Yes, he's chunky. He can't help it. Lady Gaga told me he was just born this way. Oh, and the vet said it was a venomous snakebite.

Liz's boyfriend offered that he thought it was from a water moccasin, because Cowboy bounded into the shallow pond and started limping immediately thereafter. Not to gross you out too much, but that weekend, the normally two-acre pond was down to about a hundred square feet and was a teeming, concentrated, writhing black mass o'moccasins. Ick.

The poor tubby baby. He didn't like the footbath. Not even a giant beef-basted rawhide bone could make it more attractive to him. His foot looked like a cow's hoof, and it was only half the size it was the night before. He was hurting so much and feeling so betrayed that he wouldn't even look at me. Or touch the bone. I gave him his meds tucked in a hotdog, then squeezed ointment between his toes. I put his tube sock on over his gooey foot, then masking-taped it on. He turned his head as far away from me as he could. I got the message. Unfortunately for him, we'd have to do this twice a day, plus when he went outside he he would have to wear a baggy over his sock.

The indignity of it all. Finally, when I was done, he hid on his pillow with his bone. After a two-minute chew, he fell into a trauma-tized sleep. Sick kids and sick pets are heart-wrenching, aren't they? The vet warned us that if his foot didn't heal, Cowboy would have to have minor surgery to explore whether there was anything stuck up in his foot. But the chances of that were slim.

Weekend tally for that little Nowheresville jaunt? Close to a thousand dollars. How do I love thee, Eric and Cowboy? Let me count the one thousand ways.

FELINITY

The alarm on my phone didn't know that Adrian had died, and it dutifully chirped at 4:45 a.m. "Adrian, Charlotte, get up! Time to train! It's going to be a great day!" it seemed to say. I considered smashing it to bits.

But what day was it, even? I thought back and realized that it was Sunday, but for the life of me, I didn't know what had happened to Saturday. Wait, yes, I could remember: tears, sleeping, hugs, sleeping, and my mother taking care of all of us.

Sabrina didn't know that Adrian had died either, and I could hear her helpful meow outside the bedroom door. She took her role of morning drill sergeant to the Hanson family seriously, and she seemed to derive great joy from it, in a restrained manner befitting her felinity.

I pushed snooze. I hadn't planned for this moment. The melatonin I had taken the night before still fogged my head. What a paradox. My heart felt dead, and my brain felt like a plate of scrambled eggs, but my body tingled and itched to get up and *do* it; it was Sunday morning, and that meant bicycling was on the agenda.

Maybe it was the right thing to do: keep training for the Ironman, manage my anxiety, and take care of myself. Other than the fact that it felt wrong to be alive—much less doing this without Adrian—it was a normal activity. If I stayed in this bed any longer, in these sheets that smelled like Adrian, I would not want to get up at all.

The alarm blared again. I gave in to the obsession in a way that Adrian would have understood and appreciated. I snuck into the living room, put my beloved pink road bike on the training stand, and hopped on. The spin of the pedals and wheels matched the spin in my head. Whursh whursh whursh whursh whursh. Faster and faster, into a trance. The schedule dictated that I ride two hours this morning. I concentrated on my form, on my cadence, on not thinking at all. Whursh whursh whursh whursh whursh. I didn't have the TV on. I didn't have music. Just the sound of my own breathing and the bike going nowhere in my Houston living room at eighteen miles per hour.

Into my "not thinking at all" broke a thought. No, not a thought, more like an image that became Adrian's face. Then a sound: Adrian's voice. The image grew vivid, the sound grew louder, and they transported me back to a moment that morphed into the present.

"Get your speed up, and then lay yourself over, one arm at a time. Find your inner cat and just relax. Balance. Don't get in a hurry about it," Adrian said.

I remembered this. Adrian had been teaching me to use the aerobars on my bicycle.

"I'm off-kilter, Adrian. I'm going to fall."

As I looked back on it, I could see myself overreacting to the subtle balance shifts. A car zoomed past and surprised me, and the gust of wind nearly knocked me over.

I squealed.

He said, "You should probably sit up when cars pass us for now."

"I can handle it."

He chuckled. "Yes, I know you can."

I froze his face in my mind, lingering on each laugh line and the whiskers he'd missed in his hasty morning shave. *Oh, Adrian. Adrian.*

Sabrina hopped up on a bookshelf and watched me expectantly. Adrian's image flickered and died. I turned my attention to the cat.

"You're the only one I didn't tell, aren't you, Sabrina?" I asked. "I'm sorry, you're part of the family, and you have a right to know. Adrian is not with us anymore." Tears joined the sweat dripping off my face. "He's not just on a trip. Don't be mad at him." Sabrina would bite our ankles whenever we had the gall to leave the house overnight. "I'm going to need you to snuggle Natalie and Sam a whole lot more. Remember that dog in Peter Pan? Nana? Well, you need to be like that dog. Protect them."

The cat's demeanor didn't change, but she didn't break eye contact either.

"I don't think I'm going to need your help, though. I'm a strong woman, Sabrina. Worry about the kids. I'll be fine." I needed to practice saying this. Why not start with the cat? "Really, I will. I will be fine. I will be fine. I will be fine. I will be fine."

I kept whispering the words over and over, fast in time with the pedal strokes. *I am so very not fine.*

PART THREE: ZOMBIELAND

LADIES AND GENTLEMEN,
MAY I HAVE YOUR
ATTENTION, PLEASE?

I t turned out that two dogs just weren't enough.

Weighing in at a full 6.5 pounds, Petey at three months was a dead ringer for Dumbo. He is a Boston terrier, although we suspected a Chihuahua got in on the action at some point in his lineage. I gave him to Eric—who was in the dumps in the wake of his youngest birth-child's departure for college—to cheer him up, after he hinted for only four months. Eric also tried to snow me into a miniature potbellied pig. I didn't feel *that* sorry for him. He had to settle for Petey.

We'd selected the Boston terrier for its short hair and size, but I had to find the perfect specimen for Eric: a calm and diminutive dog with a white face and a dark body. Calm was a must, because Eric had once had a Boston terrorist. Bowie was the Tasmanian devil, and an escape artist to boot. Petey is super calm {Everyone who has ever owned a Boston terrier is laughing their asses off here.} and a world-champion snuggler.

Cowboy and Layla took their time forgiving us. Petey is smaller than Cowboy's head, so we wooed Cowboy first, hoping to make Petey a friend, rather than a snack. We presented Cowboy with a giant yellow squeaky duck and a few treats, and that seemed to get him over the hump.

Eric wanted everyone to know right off the bat that, no matter what she thinks, this will never be Susanne's dog. He whispered, "Susanne's a big meanie," in Petey's sleeping ear over and over. It didn't help, but it made Eric feel better.

BITTEN BY THE FIVE-SECOND RULE.

I adhere to the five-second rule—not because I have children, but because when my brother Bruce and I dropped something edible on the ground when we were kids, my father would say, "It's Vitamin D." As in dirt. "Good for you." In hindsight, I know that he instructed us thusly because he is a ~~tight-ass~~~~cheapskate~~ frugal soul who worried about ~~starving children in India~~~~his wallet~~ our planet.

For my twenty-seven years alive (plus a few), I have put the five-second rule into practice with no mishaps. This recently ended in tragedy.

I was writing. I like to reward myself with snacks while I write. Write one hundred words, get a cookie, write one hundred words, have some ice cream, write one hundred words, book my liposuction. And so on.

I was noshing from a bag of expensive school-fundraiser whole salted cashews. Not only were they worth their weight in gold, but the little suckers tasted much better than my generic brand cashew pieces. Heaven.

When a cashew spurted out of my hand and hit the floor across the room, I thought, *Hmmm, I'll get that next time I'm up.* Later, I did just that. I looked down at the floor and saw what I believed to be a broken piece from my whole, yummy salted cashew. I popped it in my mouth and chomped.

Only it wasn't a cashew.

It took only one chew to know **for sure** THIS WAS NO FREAKIN' CASHEW. It didn't crunch like a cashew, it stuck to my teeth, and it didn't emit that oily, salty goodness of cashew.

Gwack. Gwack. Gwack. I started gagging before I reached full speed as I careened through the house. Gwack. Gwack. Gwack.

"Mom, what's wrong?!?" Clark asked.

Gwack.

"Honey?" Eric said.

Gwack.

By now a three-foot-long drool trail streamed behind me, and I foamed from the corners of my mouth. I reached the kitchen sink and started splashing water up into the accident site. Splash. Swish. Spit. Splash. Swish. Spit.

"Pamela, what ARE you doing?" Eric asked.

I tested my progress by gently closing my mouth until my teeth met. GWACK. It was still there. It was like I had bird poo—crunchy on the outside, gooey-sticky in the center—molded and stuck against my tooth. GWACK.

I reached back to my molars and scraped frantically with my fingernail, trying to get *whatever it was* off my teeth. Something that tasted nothing like cashews (*don't think about it*) fell from my tooth onto my tongue. GWACK. Splash. Swish. Spit.

Clark and Eric both stood beside me now, their eyes wide, helpless to figure out what was going on, unable to assist, Eric with one hand on speed dial for the wacky ward.

"Five second rule—not a cashew—stuck to my teeth," I gasped.

I dashed to the bathroom, desperate to unload the full force of my Braun Oral-B Triumph and half a tube of Colgate Total on this bad boy. *Ahhhhhhhhhhhhhh.*

By now, my devoted husband and son were also in the bathroom. You might imagine them expressing concern or running for the ipecac, but no. I think Eric actually peed himself laughing, and Clark, all 5'11" of him, rolled around in the bathroom floor howling, crying —real tears, I swear—and pointing at me.

When Eric had changed his drawers and resumed his composure, he said, "I'll bet you wish you hadn't gotten rid of the cleaning service two months ago."

Yes, that is how long it has been since anyone cleaned the floor in question. I'm a writer, a mom, a wife, an attorney, a consultant, an athlete, but I am NOT a housekeeper.

"Mom, what if it's from one of the dogs or Juliet?" Clark asked.

Gwack.

I know what my dad would say: "Hopefully it was a good source of protein."

THE PAIN OF PUPPY LOVE

How quickly Eric's little Boston terrier became the canine love of my life. It took, what, one week? I knew I loved him madly, but I did not grasp the depth until one Thursday at 6:45 a.m.

I was in the kitchen with Petey, who had stopped bounding around the house like a bunny rabbit with his ears pinned back long enough to gobble his Fromm's gourmet puppy food, milk, and chicken, that I'd warmed up to the perfect temperature for his eating pleasure. Clark and Susanne were shoveling muffins down like zombies. Our big dogs were wolfing their breakfasts about thirty feet away, down a long hall and in another room.

And then I heard one angry snarl, followed by a squeal and frantic, breathless crying.

Petey. My sweetie Petey.

I ran toward the big dog area, my mind whirling. Hadn't Petey been at my feet? How could he have made it back there so fast with none of us seeing him?

When I got to the room, I saw that Petey had scrambled under the electric piano, and his cries ripped through my gut. Our beloved Cowboy was on his belly, crawling toward me in supplication.

"BAD DOG," I yelled, and whacked him. I didn't have to see it to know what had happened. Petey had come between 125-pound

Cowboy and his food bowl. If there's one thing Cowboy loves, it's food. Layla normally waits to eat until Cowboy is done, because she doesn't want him to even think she's after his chow.

"Petey, Petey sweetie, come here," I cooed, and crawled after him as he ran from me, crying, under tables, chair, and piano. I was faster, and I soon scooped him up to soothe him. I held him to me, and his cries lessened.

"What did he do? What did Cowboy do to him?" Clark yelled, and he grabbed Cowboy and held him to the floor.

"He got upset when Petey tried to eat his food, but I already took care of it."

"Don't hurt Cowboy," Susanne yelled at Clark.

Clark couldn't help it. Petey's yelps were tearing all of our hearts. Cowboy took another few lumps, and Clark put the big dogs outside.

That's when I saw it.

The room was dark—it was early, there were no lights on yet—and I had not seen any damage, so I assumed Cowboy had been all bark and no bite. But I was wrong.

Petey's bloody eye had popped out of its socket and was hanging from his face.

I screamed. I sobbed and ran for our bedroom with Petey in my arms, yelling for Eric, my mind white with panic. I don't remember what I was saying. I think I said, "Cowboy's hurt him. Cowboy hurt Petey badly. He's hurt. He's hurt bad." Something like that. Over and over.

Eric was in the shower. He ran out in a towel, and the look I saw on his face matched the anguish I felt.

"I don't know what to do, Eric," I cried.

"I don't either." He pulled off his towel and wrapped it around our whimpering, shivering baby.

"I'll find a vet," I said, and I started simultaneously Googling for emergency vet services and telling Eric what happened. I wrote down a number incorrectly, wasted time retracing my steps, and finally reached a vet who talked me through what to do. There was a clinic five minutes away that opened in twenty.

"Is he in shock?" I asked as I pulled clothes onto my husband.

Eric held Petey tight against his chest. "I don't know. We just need to get him to a vet as fast as we can," Eric said.

We sprinted through the house with both teenagers and Clark's girlfriend Allie, who had arrived during the pandemonium, on our heels.

I spoke through shaking lips, through my tears. "You can bike or walk to school. I'll get you an excuse note later. We have to take Petey to the hospital."

Three stricken faces nodded. Susanne dissolved into sobs and put her head on the kitchen bar. There was no time to comfort her.

Eric sat in the passenger seat with Petey and I immediately took a wrong turn out of the driveway.

Relax. Pull it together. Don't make this worse for Petey.

"Damn Cowboy. Stupid, stupid Cowboy," I said.

"If he had wanted to hurt him, Petey would be dead. He didn't mean to hurt him," Eric said.

I pictured our giant yellow dog on his belly, whining, crawling toward me before I had even found Petey. Cowboy. Our big yellow lab, our pet whom we loved.

"I know. I know. I know. I just hate him right now. I can't help it. He hurt Petey. And I could have stopped it. How did I let Petey out of my sight? Why didn't I feed Cowboy outside? I let this happen. Oh Petey, oh Petey." I could hardly drive, but we were almost there.

The clinic wasn't open yet, but I rang the bell anyway and a kind young man opened the front door. "Our puppy, his eye," I got out, then Eric was beside me with Petey and showed him to the man.

"His eye and his face, it's an emergency, it's bad," Eric said.

The young man nodded and ushered Eric straight back to the surgical suite as he yelled for a vet. I tried to fill out the forms but I couldn't remember the date or our zip code. Less than ten minutes later, Eric was sitting beside me and five people were clustered over Petey, taking care of him. Eric put his arms around me and I pressed my wet face into his shoulder and let my sobs bounce us in a oddly calming rhythm.

We started a dialogue by text with the kids, who had decided to wait for us and worry about truancy later. Susanne was terrified we would give Cowboy away.

Eric and I looked deep into each other's eyes, and he shook his head no.

"No. He is family," Eric typed.

Before long, the vet came with an update, then invited us back to be with our little buddy, who was under anesthesia.

"I consulted an ophthalmologist. This is the worst swelling I've ever seen. The eye was intact, but the optic nerve was damaged. It's not uncommon for breeds with flat faces and protruding eyes to have an eye pop out. Sometimes they keep their sight, sometimes not. But Petey has only about a one- to two-percent chance of seeing out of this eye. He may not even keep it. But we'll do everything we can to make both things possible, and even if we have to remove the eye later, it won't affect his quality of life. We've managed to get the eye back in the socket, but just barely. Thank goodness you were able to come quickly or we wouldn't have been able to. We've sewed it shut. His stitches will stay in for four weeks, then come out one stitch a week. You have your work cut out for you." She put her hand on Petey's side for a moment, looking at him. She explained the complicated regimen of creams, pills, and ice packs. We stroked Petey's warm body. I cried some more and a vet tech held a box of Kleenex out to me.

"Your main challenge is that in twenty-four hours, he'll want to resume normal puppyhood, and you need to keep him still enough that he doesn't pop the eye back out. Keep him away from the excitement of the big dogs as much as you can."

The big dogs. Cowboy. We had already explained how it happened. I didn't know how to reconcile Petey's eye with my love for Cowboy or my personal guilt, and frankly, I wasn't ready to do either one yet.

As if she could read my mind, she went on. "Petey acted like a terrier puppy. Cowboy acted like a normal dog. This kind of thing happens. They'll probably be best friends someday." She gestured toward Petey. "Don't be too hard on your big dog. There are no lacerations to his face or eye. It could have just popped out from a blow, like from the big dog's head, or from furniture or the wall. I've seen bug-eyed dogs like him run into walls and ruin their eyes more than once. They have no structural protection."

Images flashed through my mind in a crazy high-speed slide show. Cowboy crawling toward me on his belly. Petey's swagger as he sidled up to Cowboy and sat on his leg the night before. Petey leaping up to lick Cowboy's mouth. Petey's dangling eye and bloody face.

They brought Petey out of his anesthesia and he immediately sat bolt upright, looking loopy but ready for a fight. He got a round of laughs.

"What a tough little guy!" one of his helpers exclaimed. Yes, he was.

Four hours later, I brought Petey home. It was stressful, emotional, and very busy, and I confess, I cried for a good part of the first twenty-four hours. We had a few high-risk moments, like when Petey got excited and leaped into the air in a sideways twist and body-slammed himself bad-eye-side first into the floor. He fell into our backyard pond, completely immersing the eye I was supposed to keep dry in dirty water. He managed to sneak a back-footed scratch of his eyelid when I wasn't looking and drew blood. He beat his eye against the floor playing with Stinky Bunny. He bumped into furniture on his blind side. Over and over again, I heard his yelp of pain.

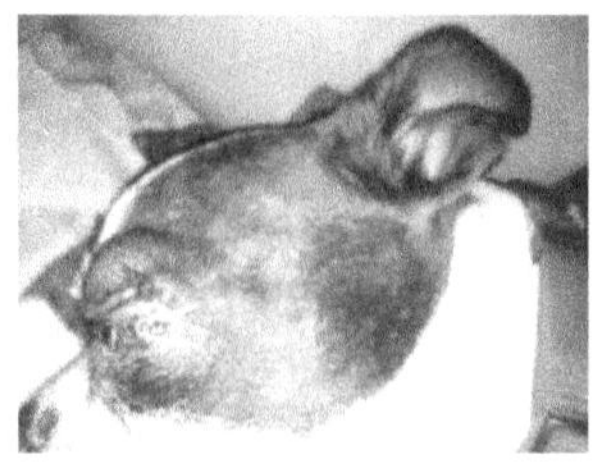

But he thrived. He ate like a champ, he tolerated his eye meds, and he gave kisses just as freely as before. He dashed around like his cranked-up jackrabbit self. He discovered that he likes the T-bones I tried to bribe him with even more than he likes Boston Market chicken. Being an injured dog had its privileges. He even got to sleep in our bed so I could keep him from scratching.

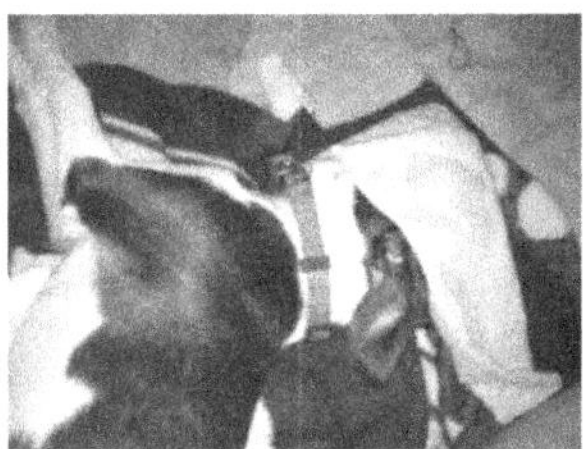

Above: Teeny-tiny ice pack.

And the biggest thing? The thing that made heart swell like a water balloon in my chest? Cowboy. Yes, Cowboy.

Cowboy was banished to the backyard for a full twenty-four hours post-incident. I couldn't even look at him. It took Eric three full days to speak to him. Susanne pleaded with us to forgive him, but just the thought of him threw me right back into the trauma.

When I let Cowboy in the house for the first time after Petey's injury, I held our little Boston in my arms. Petey with his giant swollen eye. Petey who would likely never see again from his left eye, and who would never look the same.

Above: Thirty-six hours later, with a T-bone.

Cowboy walked straight up to Petey and me, sniffed Petey and licked his face. He nudged Petey's belly with his giant muzzle. Petey was in ecstasy. His body wriggled in my arms. He strained and stretched to lick Cowboy back. Then Cowboy put his bony dinosaur head into my hand and stared up into my eyes and wagged his tail slowly. He talked to me, he cried to me in his Chewbacca language. Can a dog feel remorse and ask for forgiveness? This one sure seemed to.

I put Petey on the ground and he pogoed up to kiss Cowboy. Cowboy hung around for some Petey love for a moment, then ambled off to lie down in his favorite spot.

Someday they will be best friends. Petey will be fine. If their hearts were big enough to love past that horrible, traumatic incident —that tragedy—then mine was, too. Puppy love. We've got it bad.

I ♥ Petey, the slightly-less-beautiful-than-before dog. I love him even more than I did when he had two big black eyes that shone with mischief. In fact, I love him twice as much with one eye as I did with two.

And I love the big yellow dog; I have since he was our silly puppy. I always will.

A WAKING DREAM

Excerpt from the novel *Finding Harmony (Katie #3) {We goin' back to de islans, mon}*:

A hand touched my shoulder, then pushed it. "Katie? Katie, wake up. It's me," Nick said.

I fought waking, but my eyes opened after he had shaken me a few more times. "What time is it?" I asked.

"It's three a.m. I know it's late, but I need to tell you something."

"Where have you been?" I asked.

"Don't you remember, silly? I went shopping for presents to make you smile."

"Oh, yeah. You told me that."

My eyes closed. His hand shook my shoulder again.

"Katie, wake up, listen to me, because I can only talk for a moment. I need you to know I am all right. Don't stop looking for me. Take the picture with you. I'm counting on you."

"Wait! What? Nick?" I jumped up, the cotton sheets sliding to the floor as my feet hit it. "Nick?"

Nick was not there. Of course he wasn't. *You're dreaming*, I thought as I climbed back into bed, tears falling. *It was just a dream.*

Crash. I jumped. Annalise's agitation sparked in the air around me, and I realized she had hurled something to the ground. I got out of bed again, and this time I flipped on the light switch. The sound had come from Nick's closet. I opened the door.

His tackle box sat upright on the floor, five feet down from its shelf above Nick's hanging clothes rack. *What do you mean, Annalise? A tackle box?*

I squatted down beside it and placed both my hands on its lid. I closed my eyes. "I'm all right. Don't stop looking for me. Take the picture with you. I am counting on you." Nick's voice filled not just my head but my whole body.

I opened the box and pulled out each item, one by one. Hooks, leaders, and rubbery squid. Odds and ends I couldn't name. And a picture. A water-damaged picture of Nick and his father on a fishing boat. The Little Mona Lisa. "What is this? Annalise, Nick? What am I supposed to get from this? Annalise? Help me, please help me." Stillness. Complete quiet.

After several long minutes sitting on the floor in front of Nick's closet waiting for an answer or an idea, I gave up. I tucked the picture into my travel bag, and returned to bed. I slept the last hour and a half, but not well, Nick's voice and Annalise's antics in my head.

By five a.m., Kurt and I had grabbed the coffee cups Ruth held out for us, and I had pointed the nose of the Silverado toward the airport. We sipped our coffee in silence as we drove to catch our flight.

Nick, I'm coming to find you.

PUPDATE

Despite the full-time job that is nursing a Boston terrier puppy through a devastating eye injury, my world kept revolving on its axis. I was thankful, though, that the client I'd had scheduled for the next week called to reschedule. God granted me time to keep an ice pack on Petey's eye during his naps. But not much time.

Clark qualified for the state tournament in cross-examination debate, Susanne swam two swim meets (and won the 500 free in one of them) and sang in her first choir concert, Liz celebrated fall break with the season's first snow and a bear on campus, and Thomas visited us (yay!). Only Marie required no special attention, which earned her favorite-child status for the week.

I got a rejection letter from an agent after a nearly five-month-long review of one of my novels. Since this happened on the afternoon of the day Petey hurt his eye, it didn't impact me as much as past rejections have. Instead, it fueled my conviction that traditional publishing is on its way out. I am embracing the new era. And icing Petey's eye.

Above: "I fought the pig, and the pig won."

About one week after Petey's injury, we took Petey, Layla, Cowboy, and JuJu to the vet all at the same time. Those four, plus Eric, Clark, Susanne, and me, all in the Suburban. It was quite a show. They're building an addition onto the clinic and naming it in our honor.

GATORAMA

I don't know what you call it where you live, but the lifestyle we call redneckin' is alive and well under many names in this fine country. In south central Colorado, for instance, we found it at the Colorado Gators Farm. So, duh, the gator farm became the total highlight of our trip.

We came to be in the vicinity of said gator farm while visiting our daughter Liz, whose college is nearby. In other words, the gator farm is so awesome that whole towns and universities have sprung up around it. It's like the cultural spoke in the wheel of SoCo.

It didn't start that way. Originally, the gator farm was a tilapia farm perched (get it?) atop a natural hot spring. While fancy fish can survive in cold and even frozen water, it turns out they like eighty-seven degrees way better. This little nugget of information raised my respect for fish intelligence tenfold.

The first gators at the farm were nothing more than green garbage disposals: they ate the dead fishies. Dead fishies stink, and aren't good for much else than feeding gators. The founders of the gator-Dispose-All concept were so forward-thinking in their green-ness, in fact, that they didn't even buy the gators. They recycled the cast-off gators that no one else wanted. So if you ever wondered where those cute little caiman gators at the local pet shop ended up, I'll tell you: they're freezing their asses off eating dead tilapia in SoCo.

When we visited, it was a balmy nine degrees outside, and the gators were "resting." Even water bubbling up at eighty-seven degrees from down below gets a bit nip when it's that cold outside. This makes the gators very, very sleepy. Did you know a gator can survive while frozen? It can. Not for all that long, but the record at the gator farm is forty days after a good freeze for a gator to emerge, thaw, and resume somewhat normal brain function, which wasn't all that much to begin with.

I don't want to suggest that working at the gator farm is high-risk, but we did see three different memorial posters to employees who had died prematurely, cause of death unknown. Two brave gator wranglers remained when we were there. I think the stress of their jobs may have gotten to them a little. About all they wanted to talk about was duck rape {OK, y'all, as a victim of sexual assault myself years ago, I know rape is a serious topic. And that's exactly why it is odd and thus ultimately funny that they brought it up and talked about it at length with my two teenage daughters present.}. If you haven't yet had the opportunity to explore the social crisis that is the rape of defenseless female ducks, I highly recommend a tour of the Colorado Gators Farm.

There was way more to see than just gators (and hydroponic farming and tilapia tanks) at the gator farm. For instance, we saw a biodome. It reminded me of Mad Max and the Thunderdome, except smellier. A whole lot smellier. We also enjoyed the rescued tortoises, snakes, geckos, frogs, possum, parrots, emu, goats, horses, donkeys, sheep, ostrich, and cats. Cats as in plural. Cats as in prolific breeders. Apparently the gators' diet does not include much cat. There were a lot of goats, too, and I'm pretty sure one of the donkeys was knocked up. It is possible that ducks aren't the only things getting raped at the gator farm.

No redneck story is complete without potty humor, so I want to tell you about Monster, the generously-proportioned tortoise/toilet paper roll holder. When Monster was rescued, he weighed three times what he should have, because his former owner lovingly hand-fed him meat for years. Monster hangs out by the potty so often that the handlers keep a roll of toilet paper on his back. When unsuspecting guests reach for the roll and it rises up under their hand, they run screaming and half-decent from the bathroom. Hilarious to the gator-wranglers, but not necessarily to the guests themselves.

I don't want any of this to scare you out of a visit to the Colorado Gators Farm, because it is totally worth the price of admission, if for nothing else than a chance to see Morris, the resident movie star, whose many film credits include *Happy Gilmore* and *Doctor Doolittle 2*. We didn't actually see Morris, as he has a special private gator enclosure appropriate for a star of his caliber, but we did have the *chance* to. He's (supposedly) right next to the pile of frozen gators that didn't make it past forty days, and just down the path from the bone yard of gators past, who shall rest in peace until someone requests a gator skeleton. And then, if the price is right, the wranglers will exhume the body, hose it off, and ship it UPS wherever you would like.

We loved the gator farm and made it out intact with certificates of bravery in hand for holding Albuquerque the sleepy caiman alligator, who even signed our certificates with a full imprint of his teeth. The wranglers encouraged us to come back during the summer, when they personally teach gator-wrestling lessons. I know we'll at least send Susanne, because we've had one too many tours through teenage girlhood at our house, and we were going to put her up for sale on eBay, anyway. If she survives the gator wrestling lessons, she'll have picked up some skills that we hope she will use in her dating years.

We saw *We Bought A Zoo* the night before our visit, and when we saw For Sale signs everywhere at the gator farm, we started thinking it would be a great idea ... for some other family.

FOR SALE, $5.00—ONE-EYED DOG WHO PEES ON BED

Text from actual (short-lived) ad on Craigslist:

For sale, $5 OBO, to a good home: one-eyed dog who pees on the bed. This Boston terrier puppy eats his body weight daily and later expels roughly 1.7 times that on the master bed and in high-traffic areas. He is prone to bumping into walls, bicycle stands, furniture, etc. He is excellent at finding all the tchochkes you have lost under the couch. Loves to chew and prefers things that smell like humans. A specialist at whipping the rest of the animals into a frenzied mob. A gatherer and a hoarder, he steals anything he can grip with his mouth. Oh, and he only has one working eye, but it's real pretty. His vet bills come with him. Act fast, this one won't last long at this price.

If he'd had both eyes, I'd have had to charge $10.

EWE'S NOT FAT, EWE'S JUST FLUFFY.

 ctual email:

——Original Message——
    From: Pamela Hutchins
    To: Eric Hutchins
    Subject: Petey pic
    He put the bear under his chin as a pillow himself
    Tired little bugger after playing outside

From: Eric R. Hutchins
    To: Pamela Hutchins
    Subject: Re: Petey pic

He is SOOOOOOOOOO cute, and he looks really fat in the picture
——Original Message——
From: Pamela Hutchins
To: Eric R. Hutchins
Subject: RE: Petey Pic
Maybe he had a teeny tiny snack right before the picture
Or maybe he's retaining water

FROM: Eric R. Hutchins
To: Pamela Hutchins
Subject: Re: Petey pic
You are BAAAAAAAAAAAAD
And that was funny

Above: Petey as Barbossa from *Pirates of the Caribbean: Curse of the Black Pearl*

What does a one-eyed dog who looks like a zombie wear for Halloween? Why, a zombie pirate costume, of course. And how does he celebrate Halloween? He does a lap around the vet's clinic decked out in his pirate garb, his legs outstretched in a joy-prance.

While he was there, he got another stitch out, and did great. He still had no sight in the eye, though, and because there was muscle damage and the eye was turned wrong, only the white of his eye (which was red) had been visible since the accident. Only when we put the medicine under his eyelid could we see his big beautiful iris.

His wandering eye looked Looney tunes, but with a swagger. Go, Petey.

GECKO LOVE

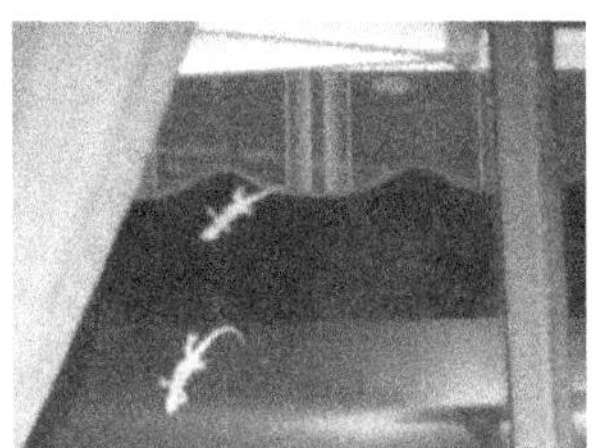

For the last year or three, a male gecko has used our master bedroom sliding glass door as his bug-hunting hang out. I adore him. Nothing defuses whatever ugly mood swing I'm experiencing faster than spying his little green body creeping on spongy toes across the glass. He only comes out at night, and only in late spring through early fall.

In the past, he was always alone. Solo gecko. A bachelor. The gecko man about town. Until June of this year. I looked up one June evening and saw the blessed sight of Mr. Gecko with a Miss, who later became his Mrs. (or at least his baby mama). I snapped this blurry shot.   Where did she come from? How did they meet? GeckoMatch.-com? Were they betrothed from birth by gecko parents eager to ensure the perpetuation of their shared genetics and culture? Or did Mr. Gecko's friends tire of his partying and set him up with a hot young thing to entice him to settle down? Whatever and however, it was gecko love.

One month later, I discovered that a tiny red gecko baby with bulbous eye-orbs under translucent lids had found his way into our master bath. We watched him until he escaped without a whisper under our cabinets. Within two weeks, I saw another of the offspring on the glass with Mom and Pop. They were all too far apart to get a snap of them together, but Pop huffed out his chest/neck in obvious pride.

How cool is gecko love?

TINY CATHOLIC

In Amarillo where I grew up, you were religiously diverse if you were anything but Church of Christ. So, as someone who was on the outside, I thought I had sensitivity for religious diversity, I thought I got it. I was raised Methodist, chose Disciples of Christ, and now go to a Baptist church. Eric has had a similar Protestant journey.

So let's just get this out there: Petey is Catholic, y'all. We found out during Lent, when he came home on Ash Wednesday with the remnants of a cross on his forehead. He'd obviously tried to scrub it off, fearing our disapproval.

We really should have picked up on it sooner, with his Boston background. And it's going to be okay—it's not like he's Pentecostal, after all. He's just a Catholic, and we're not in Amarillo anymore. We're in Houston, and there's a heck of a lot of Catholics here. It's just that most of them speak English as a second language. Come to think of it, though, English isn't Petey's first language, either.

It will be fine. Really, it will.

AT LEAST WE'LL ALWAYS BE
ABLE TO FIND IT.

Petey the one-eyed Boston terrier went under the knife for the snip-snip. You know, *neutering*. Why, you may rightly ask, would we do this to our sweetie Petey?

Well, when we picked him up from boarding at the super awesome Polka Dot Dogs two weeks before, they said, "Your little darlin' is trying to become a father and has his one eye on that Chihuahua over there. And the cockapoo. Oh, and also the Maltese."

Pooooooor Petey. In his defense, he told me all three were super hot little bitches. And he *loves* Polka Dot Dogs. Instead of kennels, they let all the dogs of similar size and temperament play in open rooms together. He'd like us to take him along wherever we go, but if he can't go with us, he prefers PDD.

PDD, however, has a policy: At the age of seven months, little boy doggies no longer get to stay in open-room boarding if they can't keep it to themselves. While I think anyone would be lucky to get the bonus of little Peteys along with the price of their boarding, I *guess* I can accept this.

So, Petey visited his very intimate buddies at the vet's office. After three months of eye treatments, they know and love him well. After neutering my poor baby, they know him even better. Before the procedure, they asked me if I'd like them to put a microchip in Petey, in case he ever gets lost. I said yes, but then I remembered that Eric and I had agreed to partner on all parenting decisions, and Petey was our newest child, after all.

I called Eric. "Do we want Petey to have one of those Pet Finder microchip thingies?"

Eric said, "Sounds like a good idea to me."

"Excellent, because I already told them yes," I confessed. "They said they can put one in when they remove his you-know-whatsies."

Eric paused. "Wait a second. They remove his you-know-whatsies and put the chip in the space left behind?"

"I didn't ask, but that sounds likely, since this only came up because of his procedure."

"So he'll have a tracker in his ball sack??"

"I wouldn't have put it quite like that, but, yeah, I guess that's about right."

Another pause.

"Well, I guess we'll always be able to find it, then," Eric said.

Ew. I'm thinking this microchip may tell us a little more than we really wanted. Whatever happened to the right to privacy? What do we do when Petey starts dating? Or, God forbid, gets married? Wouldn't it be enough of a challenge that he couldn't father little Peteys without his anxious parents tracking his every move with his beloved? Not to mention the whole one-eye thing. This is a little more intrusive than, say, a GPS tracker in a car, which I'm not above installing in my kids' vehicles if they deserve it. But a ball sack tracker? Could I do that to him?

As I pondered the horrors, Eric broke into my reverie. "I'm kidding, Pamela. It's a good idea. It's fine. I'll bet they don't even put it there. I'll bet they just use the occasion of anesthesia to tuck it in somewhere else."

"Really?"

"Really."

I exhaled. What a relief, because I was pretty sure that wherever they were going to put the microchip, it was a done deal by now.

Later that same day, I picked up our Petester. Oh, what a pitiful sight he was, head hanging, eyes downcast. He seemed awfully low, even for a dog that had lost his manhood. I paid and whisked him to the car, whispering supportive and encouraging words in his ear about his bright future and the long line of female dogs who didn't give a rat's ear about puppies, citing to our own Layla and Cowboy as examples of devoted and puppyless partners.

Nothing worked. I just couldn't cheer him up. We were almost home when a cold dread seeped over me. I pulled to the side of the road and put the car in park. I knew even before I carefully searched his sixteen-pound body for a microchip incision what I would find —nothing.

The only point of entry? Yes, you guessed it: the poochy pouch. Little tears of guilt welled up in the corners of my eyes. I stroked him and begged for his understanding and forgiveness. This appeared to mollify him a bit, and we headed for home.

As I was making dinner that night, Susanne came in. "I guess that surgery didn't work. Petey's humping his stuffed German shepherd."

A few minutes later, Clark swung by. "What a stud, Mom. Petey's giving it to that kangaroo. Didn't he just get his balls chopped off today?"

When he walked through the door, Eric exclaimed, "Wow, Petey, you aren't letting a little pain stop you, are you?"

I could only imagine. As I pondered his actions, even I had to admit it. Our Petey is a total slut. Maybe the vet put the tracker exactly where we need it to be.

ANGELS

Here on the island of Kona, I followed the training plan that Adrian had laid out for us nine months before, when he'd qualified for the Hawaii Ironman. I stayed in the Kona Awesome Condo he had rented because he got such a kick out of the name. I ate the egg-white omelet at Lava Java and passed on the coffee. No caffeine within forty-eight hours of race time, per previous instructions by Adrian. I attended all the events and expos and dinners he would have wanted to go to.

Of course, I expected that any minute now, somehow he would join me, that I would feel him, that he would be here, but he remained stubbornly absent. I coasted on autopilot, programmed to my course, and I did not give in to the pain. I felt nothing, not even scared, betrayed, or tired anymore.

Wandering through the town, I saw fliers announcing the memorial for Adrian taped up everywhere. This service sounded like a bigger deal than I had imagined it to be. I hated the thought of attending, but Adrian would have loved it. I would go for him, and behave graciously. As graciously as I could, anyway.

I walked down to St. Peter's. Adrian and I had planned to visit it together on the night before the race. The little blue clapboard church was right on Ali'i Drive, near the start/finish of the triathlon. It stood on the beach, surrounded by a lei of pink bougainvillea bushes. The setting sun cast light that filtered through the etched glass window above the doorway to the church onto the aisle between the pews in a rainbow of color.

I took my place inside.

The priest spoke to the gathered athletes. "Tomorrow you may need an angel. You will put your body and mind through an incredible test. Believe in your angel, and he or she will come to you when you need it most."

I would look for mine tomorrow, that was for sure. If I couldn't find Adrian at Kona, I didn't believe I could find him anywhere.

An older woman sitting under the third station of the cross caught my attention. "Of course," I thought. I was looking at my triathlon idol, Sister Madonna Buder, the seventy-nine-year-old Roman Catholic nun famous for completing over 325 triathlons, thirty-six of them full-length Ironmans. She didn't even start triathlon until she was fifty-two. I remembered a quote Adrian had attributed to her: "I train religiously." Now she was kneeling at the altar in St. Peter's with me.

And tomorrow was the big day. I prayed and prayed and prayed.

When the service was over, I walked out of the church and down toward the starting line, the site of Adrian's memorial. Hundreds of people were gathered there. Hundreds. I fought back the waves of emotion. *Stay strong. Not yet.*

A loud voice snapped me out of my fog. James Harvey, an Austin triathlete Adrian had known for many more years than he had known me, spoke through a bullhorn. "Thanks for coming, everyone. We are here to honor our friend, writer and fellow triathlete, Adrian Hanson. You all know Adrian. His words painted the picture of our sport. There's his beautiful wife, Charlotte, now."

James waved to me and hundreds of heads turned. I waved back, smiling gamely but glad for the growing darkness.

"If I passed the microphone around, we could spend all night here telling stories about Adrian, but Adrian would not approve of us missing our beauty sleep before the race." The crowd tittered. "Instead, volunteers are passing around Bic lighters and Sharpies.

Here's what we want you to do. Take the Sharpie and write a message to Adrian some place that won't conflict with body marking tomorrow, but make it someplace that will show. Write his name, or 'in memory of Adrian,' or some such. Whatever you want. Then, when we are all done with the Sharpies, we'll use our Bics."

The crowd hummed as people wrote on their arms and legs. I finally cried. No one had told me this was the plan. It was perfect. I wrote "For Adrian" on the sides of both my shins.

"You guys, please spread the word to everybody that couldn't be here tonight about our special body marking. I'd love to see Adrian's name plastered on every leg in Kona tomorrow, OK?"

The crowd cheered. I felt vulnerable in this teeming mass of people that had gathered to honor my husband. They engulfed me, and I lost my balance in a rush of vertigo. I wanted to reach out and hold onto the person next to me to steady myself. Better yet, I wanted to turn to find Adrian beside me and grab his arm.

"Time for lighters, everyone. So, light 'em up, hold 'em high, and let's observe one minute of silence while we remember our lost friend, Adrian Hanson, who we will forever miss."

The snapping sound of Bics lighting up resounded in hundreds of small clicks around me. I lit mine and held it aloft. The man standing next to me watched me as I swayed.

He leaned toward me and whispered, "Charlotte?"

I cocked my head in answer and nodded.

The stranger reached down and held my hand.

I struggled not to sob, to stay upright. Then the woman next to me put her arm around my waist. The minute stretched on a very long time.

"Amen," James said.

"Amen," the crowd answered.

James wrapped it up. "Thank you all for being here. Please drop your lighters and Sharpies in the boxes on the pier as you leave. Don't forget to spread the word about the extra body marking. And hold up —I almost forgot, Charlotte is here to race, keeping up the family tradition for her husband. Y'all encourage her out there tomorrow. Go get some rest, see you here tomorrow bright and early."

I turned to thank my angels, but they were gone.

TINY MUSLIM

S top the presses!

Not long ago, I confessed that Petey had converted to Catholicism during Lent. But what a difference a week made. I walked in a week later and found him in this pose. There was no yoga DVD playing to explain his body position, no reason for his devout prostration other than, you guessed it: a change of faith. Petey is now a Muslim, and below is a photograph of him praying, facing Mecca.

He needs to work on his form, methinks, but he's only an eight-month old dog. Even so, I have to wonder if his religious experimentation is genuine, or if Petey's setting me up for a discrimination charge. Maybe he's caught the lawyer ads when he watches Oprah with Susanne. I have come down on him pretty hard for his refusal to potty train, after all, and he's sharp enough to have noticed the other dogs aren't catching hell.

I'm rethinking everything now. What could he sue me for? Discriminating against him for his disability? He could have stuck his head in Cowboy's mouth intentionally. His bi-racial heritage, as evidenced by his half-black and half-white coat? Might be nothing more than a stencil, masking tape, and black hair dye on a white dog. And now? The Tiny Protestant became the Tiny Catholic who has become the Tiny Muslim. Next week I'll probably find him in dreadlocks with a yarmulke perched on his head, meditating and chanting mantras.

Or maybe I'm just paranoid. Oy vey.

COLD NOSE, WARM FEET

You know that age-old saying, "rednecking can lead to redneckedness?" Last weekend, it didn't hold any water. We spent the weekend rednecking, and there wasn't a damn bit of redneckedness.

Here's what happened. Eric and I hoofed it to Nowheresville for another idyllic weekend camped out in the Quacker. For once, I had no poo stories to bring home. Nor did I bring home any naked stories. Not that I usually share any naked stories; I'm simply confirming there were none to bring home.

And the reason for no naked stories? 1) Gas and 2) Petey, the one-eyed light of our lives. No, not *that* kind of gas. Although there was some of that, there is no causal connection between that "gas" and the "no naked" issues. Instead, I'm talking about propane gas. Eric, AKA Bubba-mon in Nowheresville, ran out of propane in our two propane tanks. Guess what kind of heater we have? P-r-o-p-a-n-e, yes.

On that same day in Houston, it was a balmy seventy degrees. But on that fateful propaneless night in Nowheresville, it got down to twenty-five. Twenty-five is a brisk daytime sunshine temp. It sucks for camping, however. Which is what you are doing if you are in the wilderness with no heater, even if you are on a mattress in a trailer.

So, for starters, it was wayyyyyyyy too cold for naked. It was flannel-jammies-double-comforter cold in the Quacker. But I mentioned reason number two for no naked: Petey.

Since it was just the right temperature for the abominable snowman, but not for a sixteen-pound dog with a thin layer of hair, Petey did not find his own bed a satisfactory place to spend the night. Actually, Cowboy and Layla didn't, either; they were living the high life in the back of the old Suburban. Don't scoff. There's a big difference between the windless inside of a vehicle warmed by their breath—and away from the yelps of coyotes and calls of the wild hogs—and twenty-five degrees on the ground outside the Quacker. Worry not, friends, the broken seals around the windows gave them ample oxygen as well.

Where was I? Oh, no naked and Petey. So Petey suggested that he join us under the double comforters in our bed. Normally, Petey is a no-people-bed kind of dog, although not for lack of trying. He only spent a night on the bed with us once before, and that was the first night after Cowboy put Petey's eye out. You would have let the little bugger sleep with you that night, too, I guarantee.

On this night, as we breathed whole storm systems of frost clouds over our heads, I felt sorry for Petey.

"Just for tonight," I said.

"Just for tonight," Eric agreed without hesitation.

We didn't even have to say, "Come, Petey." He sensed the change and leaped up between us, where he tunneled under the covers to the foot of the bed. I couldn't have asked for more. My feet were blocks of solid ice, and his warm little body thawed them right out.

As Eric and I finished Eskimo kissing goodnight a few moments later, though, a rocket shot out from under the covers, and when we pressed our lips together for a people kiss, Petey's cold, wet nose and wetter tongue made contact with both of our lips. It may not have been the most romantic way to end the evening, but I'd trade my cold feet for his cold nose anytime. So, after a few dry heaves, we bid our little critter a fond goodnight and fell asleep three abreast, all snuggled up and warm as a summer day.

RUNNING OUT OF TIME

Cowboy, our big yellow dog, the mutant labrador, the dainty little waif who talks like Chewbacca and steals hearts like a master thief . . . Cowboy is no longer a young dog. Now, after a weekend in Nowheresville, he lay at my feet. Occasionally he moaned. If I talked to him, he answered in what could best be called a wail. Our last visit wasn't such a tough weekend for him, comparatively, but every weekend of physical activity is hard now. The temperature stayed cool, which helped, and we walked more than ran, which did, too, but the end result was the same: an old, arthritic dog, heavy on his feet and feeling the passage of every day.

Once upon a time, Cowboy ruled the rainforest of St. Croix. He was master of his domain and a pack of six dogs at Estate Annaly. He ate up the ten-mile runs Eric and I took along Scenic Road overlooking North Shore on the west end of the island. He lived the life, man, he lived the life. He had his own swimming pool out back and a pond out front, and took trips to the beach every weekend. He regularly made the magic hike up the stream to Caledonia Springs. How could it get any better?

Then we moved him to Houston, to a city-sized backyard whose ponds were barely deep enough for wading. He was little more than a captive there. "Don't worry," we told him, "we promise this isn't the end. We'll find you a new home to rival Annaly someday." He wagged his vase-breaking bass drum mallet of a tail in understanding. He trusted us to make it right.

Oftentimes, though, we would pull up in our driveway to see his huge mournful head behind the bars of the gate, only his long nose sticking out. Even if he went for a run, it was on a leash, his feet pounding the concrete. Years passed this way. He made the best of it. He held it in. But he had lost so much, and the clock ticked forward steadily.

We bought sixteen acres in Nowheresville, a beautiful place. He would cry with joy when we pulled up to its gates in the old Suburban. From our earliest days there, though, it was clear he had lost a step. The charm of the place wore thin after a few hours. He'd limp around on city paws. He would stay curled up in the shade rather than join Layla in a game of chase-the-Suburban or on a forest explorations. He lost a fight with a water moccasin, although even that couldn't stop him for long.

We plan to build our someday house there and make a permanent move when our youngest child graduates from high school. Susanne the Dog Whisperer, Susanne, Cowboy's best friend. Only one problem, though: Cowboy will be nearly fourteen years old by then, which is ninety-eight in normal dog years, and nigh impossible in giant mutant labrador years.

Only a few months ago, we had allowed him to join us on a seven-mile run. It was 6:30 a.m., but it was summertime Texas. Ninety degrees and humidity were too much for him. He crawled under our Suburban, which we had parked at the halfway point, and lapped up all the water and ice from our open cooler. Layla galloped along beside us. He watched silently, licking his sore paws and panting in the heat. Earlier that same summer when we had gone for a run, Cowboy simply laid down in the road three long miles from home and would go no further. We had no way to help him except to continue on without him back to our vehicle, then return to cart him home. We found him one and a half miles from our property, laying in the muddy bottoms of an empty pond. Eric coaxed him back to the Suburban and lifted his limp, stank, and steamy body waist-high and into the truck bed.

Just last weekend, Cowboy had stumbled along the loamy trail at the end of our single file line: he brought up the rear, then me, then Layla, the ever-vigilant guard dog and accomplished runner, who was lagging well behind Petey, the sixteen-pound distance terrier who had churned out the canine equivalent of a ten-mile run twice over the Christmas holidays. Petey, the dog I had thought too small to run more than a mile or two with us. Petey, with his one eye and giant swagger, was, in a twist of fate so painfully ironic that the angels wept, the heir apparent to the kingdom of the giant yellow dog who had stolen his eye. To the home Cowboy was to have at Nowheresville, the home that should have replaced his beloved Annaly, but maybe never will. Layla will grow old there. Petey will spend his prime there, a runty little dog no match for a coyote or wild pig. But Cowboy, who in his best days could have kicked the coyote's ass and still had enough left in him to give the hog a thrashing? These shorts visits may be all he has. For Cowboy, the dog that ran rings around life and all of us on St. Croix, is running out of time.

So, God, my God and the God of all creatures great and small, if I could ask for just one thing of you for our old friend, it is this: Please let Cowboy stay with us long enough to spend peaceful evenings in front of a Nowheresville fireplace, knowing he has made it back to the promised land of a home fit for a kingly beast, a real home at last. Amen.

If God doesn't see fit to grant this prayer, I comfort myself with this thought: I've come to believe that there is so much more out there beyond myself and what my eyes can see. I wouldn't be surprised at all if Cowboy accompanies us to Nowheresville, no matter how he has to get there. And if I can remember that there is life outside the center of the universe that is me and my perceptions, I'll bet I find him there.

Someday.

EXCERPT FROM HOW TO SCREW UP YOUR KIDS

Despite Our Best Efforts

I t's not that we didn't try to screw this parenting thing up. By all rights, we should have. We did everything that we possibly could that we weren't supposed to do. We gave them refined sugar when they were babies, didn't enforce nap times, spoiled them with expensive and unnecessary gifts. We said yes when we should have said no. We said no when we should have said yes. Our swear jar was always full.

Oh, yeah. And we were one of those "blended families"—you know the kind, the ones with broken homes, divorces, stepparents and complex custody arrangements. Those people. The ones other parents are leery of, like divorce is a communicable disease or something. Who knows? Maybe it is. My own parents even told me once that I had made my children a statistic by choosing to divorce their father. That I had created an at-risk home environment for them.

Me? Perpetual overachiever, business owner, attorney, former cheerleader and high school beauty queen? The one who's never even smoked a cigarette, much less done drugs? My husband? Well, he's the more likely candidate for an at-risk homemaker. Surfer, bass player, triathlon enthusiast. Oh yeah, and chemical engineer and former officer of a ten-billion-dollar company—but you know how those rock-n-rollers are. We probably teeter somewhere between the Bundys and the Cleavers.

But there we were, watching yet another of our kids cross yet another stage for yet another diploma, with honors, with accolades, with activities—with college scholarships, no less. Yeah, I know, yadda yadda yap. There we were, cheering as the announcer called Liz's name. Three of her four siblings rose to clap, too. The fourth one, Thomas, couldn't make it because he was doing time in the state penitentiary in Florida. (Just kidding. He had to work. At a job. That paid him and provided benefits.)

We tried our best to screw it up. We had the perfect formula. But we didn't—not even close. Somehow two losers at their respective Round Ones in love and family unity got it close to perfect on Round Two. By our standards, anyway. Because we didn't give a good goldarnit about anyone else's.

What's more? We got it right on purpose. We made a plan, and we executed the plan. And it worked. After all that effort to screw things up, after the people in our lives who loved us most wrung their hands and whispered behind our backs (and those who didn't love us chortled in anticipation of our certain failure), we went out and done good.

Now, I'm no expert on child rearing (although I've had lots of practice), but I am an expert in helping grownups play nice and behave at work. How annoying is that? I know. I'm a scary hybrid of employment attorney and human resources professional, blended together to create a problem-solving HR consultant. And from where I sat, our blended household—or blendered family, as we call it—looked a lot like a dysfunctional workplace in our early days.

Or a little warren of guinea pigs on which I could conduct my own version of animal testing.

The HR principles I applied at work were, in theory, principles for humans, humans anywhere. Blendering occurs in workplaces when a leadership team gets a couple of new members, and it happens in a home with kids from different families of origins. HR principles = people principles = *blendering* principles. Right? That was my theory, anyway.

Statistics tell me that you, dear reader, are or will be in similar straits: divorced, starting over, trying to make it work. If you've already been there and done that, I hope you've disappointed all your naysayers, too. You'll enjoy this book all the more as you relate to the pains and the joys of blended families. But if you're on the cusp of what feels like an express train descending into hell and wondering how to buy a ticket back, I can help you.

Really.

Okay, probably.

If not probably, then quite possibly.

At the very least, maybe I can say I warned you, or made you laugh. It's a crazy and unpredictable ride, but the destination is worth it.

How did the Bradys do it?

Blendering Principle #1: It's hard to get anywhere if you don't know where you're going.

Most of the members of my generation know all we need to know about blended families from the Brady bunch, right?

Not.

Please, folks. That was just a sappy television show, and didn't Florence Henderson have an affair IRL {In real life.} with one of the TV sons? Sounds a lot like incest to me. We clearly need a new set of role models, yet I'd be vacationing in Fiji right now if I had a nickel for every time someone said to me, "Oh! You're just like the Brady Bunch!"

The Bradys wove their magic through engaging scripts and clever sets, cute young actors and the star power of Florence Henderson. Eric and I didn't have those crutches to lean on. Neither will you.

Real blended families start with two adults who want to pledge their troth, which in English means they want to marry. Or at least cohabitate with commitment. Oh, hell, maybe not even that. But that conundrum brings us to the genesis of our blended family success, and IMHO {In my humble opinion. Seriously, folks, get with the pop culture.}, a critical element.

Each of our kids had already endured one familial breakup. Were we ready to provide them stability and an example of enduring love? If not, why would we knowingly put them through sure trauma again? Nothing is certain in life, but Eric and I were all in. Not only were we all in, but we both had a consuming desire to demonstrate to our children the type of relationship we dreamed of for them, and neither of us felt like we had done so in our past lives. Scratch that. We absolutely *knew* we had not done so in our past lives.

So, we were madly in love and promised forever. Believed forever. Were confident in forever.

Still, this left a lot up to chance.

Pretend for a second that you married a touchy-feely HR consultant. Imagine that she had a penchant for things like mission, vision, and values statements. Picture her love of goal-setting and accountability. Some of you have mentally drawn up your divorce papers already.

Eric didn't. He and I created a relationship operating agreement (ROA) for ourselves as a couple. I may or may not have promised years of sexual favors to secure his participation, but his attitude about the project was good. Now, this isn't a relationship book. Well, it is, in a way. It is a book about our relationships with our children within a blended family. But it is not a couples' relationship book, so I'll spare you the gory details behind the ROA.

While we entered into our ROA to make our great relationship stronger, we did so knowing it would set the framework for co-parenting. Why? Because our kids were the most important things to each of us, besides one another. And since most second marriages break down over issues of stepparenting, money, or sex. Hell, many first marriages crash and burn on those issues. We had less than ideal co-parenting relationships with our exes, for sure.

So here's how our ROA looks:

Our (Exceptionally Wonderful) Marriage
Mantra: Make it all small stuff.

Our relationship's purpose is to create a loving, nurturing, safe environment that enables us to

• make a positive, joyful difference in each other's lives,

• respect each other's needs and differences,

• encourage each other's spiritual, emotional, and physical needs and development,

• practice caring, open communication,

• role-model loving relationships to our children, and

• work as partners when we parent and make major decisions.

Because we recognize that life is not always about the incredible highs, we are committed to these strategies:

• Stop, breathe, and be calm.

• Allow ourselves to cherish and be cherished.

• Be positive. Assume a positive intent and give a positive response. Speak your mind as positively as possible.

• Be reasonable. Am I being oversensitive? Am I dragging my own issues in unnecessarily?

• Be considerate. Is there anything to gain from what I am about to say? Is this the right time to say it?

• Be respectful. Don't mope, don't name-call, don't yell, don't be sarcastic.

• Be open. Explain your intent.

• Be present. Don't walk away, physically or emotionally.

• Be aware of time and energy. After 60 minutes, stop talking. Schedule another conversation for 24 hours later if there's no resolution.

• Make it safe to cry "calf rope."

• *Be* it. Do the behaviors you're seeking in each other within an hour of the first conversation.

• Be loving. Don't go to bed angry or with things unresolved.

He asks of her:

• Trust and have faith that I love you, enough that we don't have to solve everything the second it happens

• Assume a positive intent

• Listen, don't interrupt

• Don't be sarcastic

She asks of him:

• Come back to me faster and don't drag things out, because I need you

- Speak your mind assertively, and don't be sarcastic
- Don't assume the actions I take are always because of you
- Assume a positive intent

We didn't get this smart on our own. Both of us were trained to draft this type of agreement in our work lives, one of us more than the other. I specialize in working with hyper-competitive, confident-bordering-on-egomaniacal executives who are somewhat lacking in people skills, so I've spent years mediating, soothing, recalibrating, and at times walloping high-level business people into line. One of the best tools to get all the warring co-workers from different backgrounds to reach détente is an operating agreement. Even better? An operating agreement grounded in shared values, vision, and mission.

This worked so well for me with one of my problem executives that we ended up married. In fact, you just read our operating agreement.

Blendering Principle #2: Your mom was almost right: Do unto others as *they* would have done unto them.

So we addressed parenting, but more importantly, we addressed how we would handle ourselves in situations of higher stress and greater conflict. All of our commitments about behavior applied equally to the parenting context. Now, when a parent/stepparent decision point arose, we could act in accordance with pre-agreed principles.

Or we could try.

Execution got a little sloppy at times. When it did, we always had the agreement to return to, a touchstone, a refocusing point, a document which reminded us that for all we didn't agree on, there was oh-so-much-more that we did.

We filtered our day-to-day co-parenting decisions through this model. Chores, allowances, length of skirts, cell phones—you name it, we used it. Even better, we used it when we designed our family structure and plan. Did I mention I believe in planning? I believe in plans. And I believe in modifying the plan within the context of agreed principles when new circumstances arise. We got the chance for a lot of planning and re-planning, right from the start.

When Eric and I first married, his eldest son Thomas had graduated from college and had a real job, Eric's middle daughter Marie was entering college in the South, and his youngest daughter Liz lived with her mother on the East Coast. My Susanne was in elementary school, and my ADHD son Clark was in middle school; they split their time between their father and me. Our original parenting plan called for the two youngest kids to live mostly with us, for Liz to visit frequently, and for us to see Marie and Thomas as often as possible.

We envisioned all of our children, and someday their children, in our home as frequently as we could get them there. We bought a house in a great school district in Houston, with a veritable dormitory of four bedrooms upstairs and our master bedroom on the far side of the downstairs—because we love our kids even more from a distance. And how could we resist this house? It has a lush back yard with a three-level pond full of fat goldfish and koi that reminds us of the home we left behind on St. Croix in the U.S. Virgin Islands.

Just as this is not a book about couples' relationships, it is also not a book about divorce or custody battles. I could dish on those, but I won't, because even though I've changed the names of all parties in this little tome to protect the innocent[footnote]Criteria that requires Eric and me to use our real names.[/footnote], some things should and will remain private. They were painful. Isn't that the case in all divorces? You don't divorce because the relationship exceeded your expectations. You don't divvy up with a light heart the time you will spend with children you cherish. Most of you don't, anyway, and we sure didn't.

So, for whatever reason, within four months of "I do," Liz had taken up primary residence with us in Texas, and a year later Marie transferred to a university two hours away. I had never pictured myself taking a role of such primacy with two teenage stepdaughters. Teenage girls get a bad rap for good reason. It's not the easiest time in their lives, or the easiest time for the people that love them, even with great girls like Liz and Marie. Yet this new arrangement fit the model we envisioned. We just needed to flex. A lot.

I held onto my husband's hand for dear life and sucked in one deep, cleansing breath after another. We could do this. I could do this. We would have no regrets or remorse, we would give our kids the best we could, and be damn happy doing it. Yeah!

And so, very carefully and very cautiously, we began to blender.

CLICK HERE to continue reading *How to Screw Up Your Kids.*

ACKNOWLEDGMENTS

Huge thanks to my editor Meghan Pinson, who managed to keep my ego intact without sacrificing her editorial integrity. Thanks of generous proportions to my writing group, without whose encouragement and critiques I would not be publishing this book. Mega thanks to Cowboy, Layla, Petey, Juliet, and Annalise, the stars of this book, for shining so brightly. Thanks to the power of infinity to my husband Eric, without whom I would be half of a whole. The sad and lonely half.

Finally, to each and every blessed one of you who have read, reviewed, rated, and emailed/Facebooked/Tweeted/commented about my books, I appreciate you more than I can say. Stephanie, Rhonda, Liz, and Rebecca stand above the rest here. It is the readers who move mountains for me and for other authors, and I humbly ask for the honor of your honest reviews and recommendations.

BOOKS BY THE AUTHOR

Fiction from SkipJack Publishing

THE *PATRICK FLINT* SERIES OF WYOMING MYSTERIES:

Switchback (Patrick Flint #1)

Snake Oil (Patrick Flint #2)

Sawbones (Patrick Flint #3)

Scapegoat (Patrick Flint #4)

Snaggle Tooth (Patrick Flint #5)

Stag Party (Patrick Flint #6)

Sitting Duck (Patrick Flint #7)

Skin & Bones (Patrick Flint #8)

Spark (Patrick Flint 1.5): Exclusive to subscribers

THE *JENN HERRINGTON* WYOMING MYSTERIES:

BIG HORN (Jenn Herrington #1)

WALKER PRAIRIE (Jenn Herrington #2)

THE *WHAT DOESN'T KILL YOU* SUPER SERIES:

Wasted in Waco (WDKY Ensemble Prequel Novella): Exclusive to Subscribers

The Essential Guide to the What Doesn't Kill You Series

Katie Connell Caribbean Mysteries:

Saving Grace (Katie Connell #1)

Leaving Annalise (Katie Connell #2)

Finding Harmony (Katie Connell #3)

Seeking Felicity (Katie Connell #4)

Emily Bernal Texas-to-New Mexico Mysteries:

Heaven to Betsy (Emily Bernal #1)

Earth to Emily (Emily Bernal #2)

Hell to Pay (Emily Bernal #3)

Michele Lopez Hanson Texas Mysteries:

Going for Kona (Michele Lopez Hanson #1)

Fighting for Anna (Michele Lopez Hanson #2)

Searching for Dime Box (Michele Lopez Hanson #3)

Maggie Killian Texas-to-Wyoming Mysteries:

Buckle Bunny (Maggie Killian Prequel Novella)

Shock Jock (Maggie Killian Prequel Short Story)

Live Wire (Maggie Killian #1)

Sick Puppy (Maggie Killian #2)

Dead Pile (Maggie Killian #3)

The Ava Butler Caribbean Mysteries Trilogy: A Sexy Spin-off From What Doesn't Kill You

Bombshell (Ava Butler #1)

Stunner (Ava Butler #2)

Knockout (Ava Butler #3)

Fiction from Bookouture

Detective Delaney Pace Series:

HER Silent BONES (Detective Delaney Pace Series Book 1)

HER Hidden GRAVE (Detective Delaney Pace Series Book 2)

HER Last CRY (Detective Delaney Pace Series Book 3)

HER Forgotten Shadow (Detective Delaney Pace Series Book 4)

Juvenile from SkipJack Publishing

Poppy Needs a Puppy (Poppy & Petey #1)

Nonfiction from SkipJack Publishing

The Clark Kent Chronicles

Hot Flashes and Half Ironmans

How to Screw Up Your Kids

How to Screw Up Your Marriage

Puppalicious and Beyond

What Kind of Loser Indie Publishes,

and How Can I Be One, Too?

**Audio, e-book, large print, hardcover, and paperback versions of
most titles available.**

ABOUT THE AUTHOR

Pamela Fagan Hutchins is a *USA Today* best selling author. She writes award-winning mystery/thriller/suspense from way up in the frozen north of Snowheresville, Wyoming, where she lives with her husband in an off-the-grid cabin on the face of the Bighorn Mountains, and Mooselookville, Maine, in a rustic lake cabin. She is passionate about their large brood of kids, step kids, inherited kids, and grandkids, riding their gigantic horses, and about hiking/snow shoeing/cross country skiing/ski-joring/bike-joring/dog sledding with their Alaskan Malamutes.

If you'd like Pamela to speak to your book club, women's club, class, or writers group by streaming video or in person, shoot her an email. She's very likely to say yes.

You can connect with Pamela via her website
(http://pamelafaganhutchins.com)
or email (pamela@pamelafaganhutchins.com).

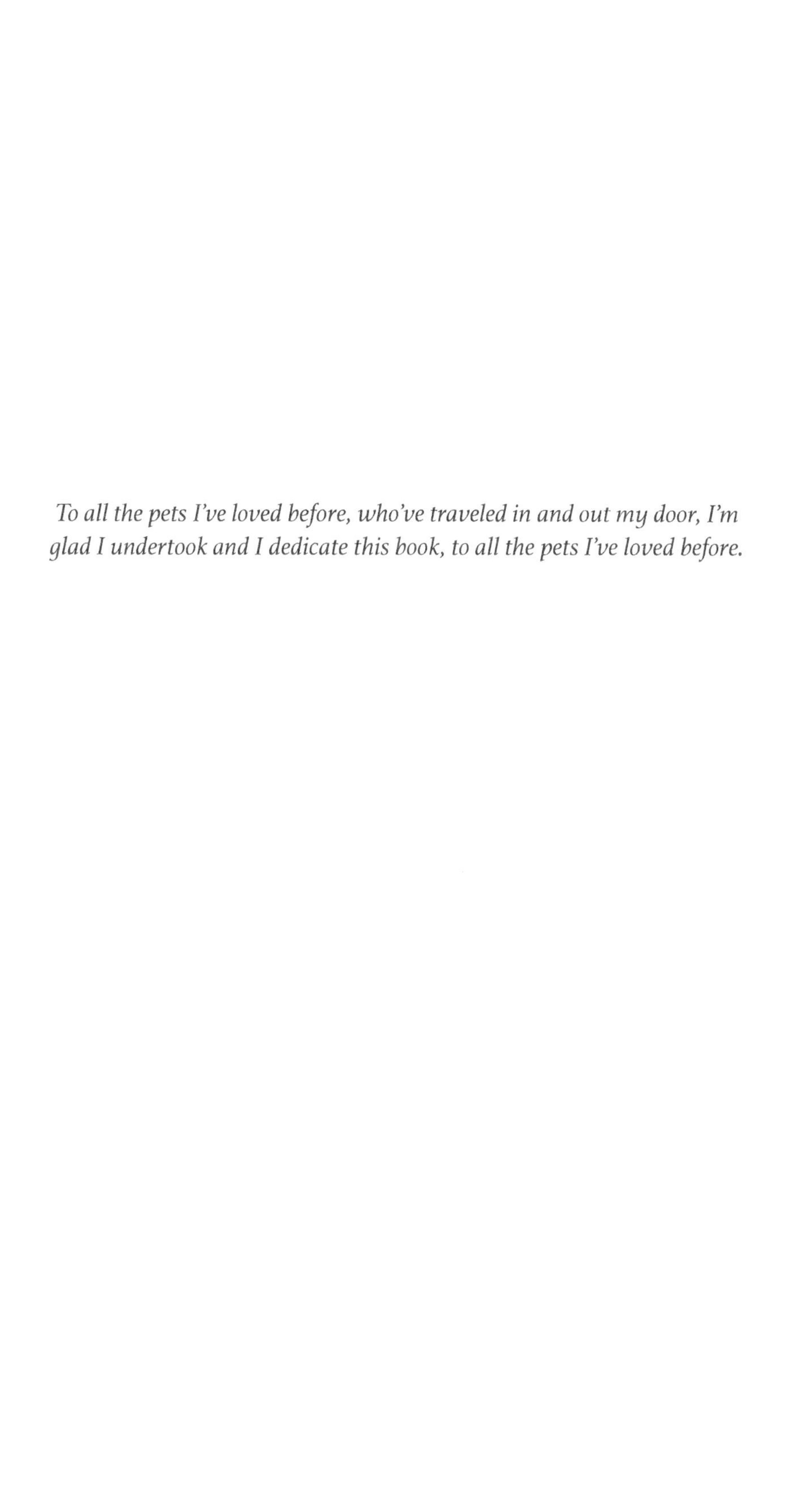

To all the pets I've loved before, who've traveled in and out my door, I'm glad I undertook and I dedicate this book, to all the pets I've loved before.

9 798227 081551